Heavenly Seas

A MEMOIR

LaCara Biddles

 FriesenPress

One Printers Way
Altona, MB R0G 0B0
Canada

www.friesenpress.com

ISBN
978-1-03-910709-0 (Hardcover)
978-1-03-910708-3 (Paperback)
978-1-03-910710-6 (eBook)

1. Family & Relationships, Death, Grief, Bereavement

Distributed to the trade by The Ingram Book Company

Table of Contents

PROLOGUE   IX

THIRTY-ONE WEEKS AND TWO DAYS PREGNANT   1

PPROM? WELL SHIT   5

CHECKING EMOTIONAL BAGGAGE   11

THE LABYRINTH OF HEALTHCARE   23

THE ULTRASOUND   29

BETWEEN TWO EVILS   35

NO TIME LIKE THE PRESENT   39
July 21, 2020, at 5:20 p.m.   40
July 23, 2020 at 9:37 a.m.   42

PRACTICE PATIENCE   45

WISHING FOR A MIRACLE   49

IT IS TIME   57

THAT IS NOT POOP   61

IT'S A GIRL   67

KAILANI MARY RANDALL   71

URNING A LIVING   81

AN ANGEL'S GIFT   87

    Numerology   88

    Angel Numbers   89

    Sweet Mama   91

    Willow Tree   92

THERE IS NO PLACE LIKE HOME   97

EMOTIONAL ROLLERCOASTER   103

IDENTITY CRISIS   111

PART 2

THE GOOD, THE BAD, AND THE UGLY OF GRIEF

THE GOOD, THE BAD, AND THE UGLY OF GRIEF   *123*

KNOW THE DIFFERENCE   125

    Mourning   125

    Grief   126

TRIGGERS OF GRIEF AND MOURNING   133

    Auditory Triggers   134

    Visual Triggers   136

    Developing New Fears   137

    Body Image   138

    Appearances   143

    Taste Triggers   143

    Grief Comparison   144

Family and Friends 146

Relationships with Significant Others 147

Counselling/Coaching 152

COMMUNICATION **155**

Retreat 156

Rethink 157

Respond 158

Awareness Wheel 159

MOURNING, GRIEF, AND SOCIETY **163**

Reactions to Grief 167

How to Support a Grieving Individual 173

Sympathy Gifts 175

Eliminate Expectations and Timeframes 176

Language 178

Save the Date(s) 183

Dos and Don'ts 183

Ring Theory 186

Communication with Supporters 189

PERMISSION TO HEAL **193**

Talk About It 197

Permission to Grieve 197

Give Back 198

Practice Gratitude 199

Mindfulness 200

Memorials 200

Journal 202

Explore Your Spirituality 203

Explore Your Creativity 203

Exercise 204

Write a Letter to Your Loved One 205

Reading 206

Take a Bath 207

A SERIES OF FIRSTS   **209**
    Facing the Holidays   210
    Facing Coworkers   214
    Returning to Work   216

PART 3

KEEPING THE MEMORIES ALIVE   *221*

FOREVER LOVED AND CHERISHED   **223**

RESOURCES   **241**
    Angel Names Association   241
    Angel Whispers Baby Loss Support Program   242
    Bridget's Cradles   242
    Center for Loss in
    Multiple Birth, Inc. (CLIMB)   243
    Empty Arms   244
    Infants Remembered in Silence (IRIS)   244
    Molly Bears   245
    Mommies Enduring Neonatal Death (MEND)   245
    Perinatal Hospice and Palliative Care   246
    Return to Zero: HOPE   246
    The Haven Network   247

ABOUT THE AUTHOR   **249**

For Kailani Mary Randall

I carried you for thirty-one weeks and five days.
I held you in my arms for only a moment.
You filled my heart like never before and left a hole
that will never be filled.

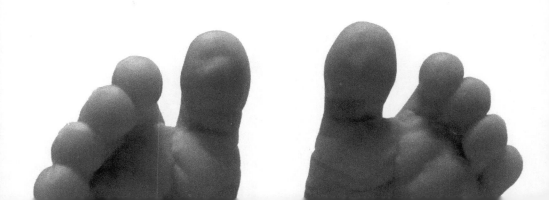

PROLOGUE

Imagine being in a room with one hundred other individuals. Someone announces that twenty-five people will be selected, at random, and receive an amazing gift. Well, in this case, we would want to be selected and would think to ourselves, *Twenty-five percent. I have a one in four shot at winning. I got this.* This is the reality that every pregnant individual face. However, we are that group of twenty-five that received the thing that nobody wants.

I would never have anticipated being in the position of writing about one of the most difficult experiences of my life. Although, I have discovered it is through these experiences of hardship and adversity that we are granted the gift of cultivating and creating a life like never before.

Going through the experience of a neonatal loss has changed me forever. There is no reality where something so heartbreaking will leave a person unchanged. For that, I am forever grateful. Because of it, I've never loved so deeply. I've never felt so connected to another soul. It's because of you, Kailani, that I am forever changed for the better.

I anticipate that if you are reading this, you too are experiencing or have experienced one of the most difficult life experiences one might live through: the death of a child. I will not say that I am sorry for your loss, because that is what society has created as the "acceptable" response to the death of a loved one. What I will say is that I am sending endless love and strength your way. I also want you to know that you have the capacity to move through your grief and continue to live a meaningful and fulfilled life. Though it may feel like life has ended or there is no point in continuing, I want you to know that this is far from the truth. You can move forward, you do have the strength, and the person you become after this will be stronger than the person you were before, as you carry the weight of this grief with you moving forward.

In the pages that follow, I share with you the most difficult and heartbreaking experience of giving birth to my beautiful daughter Kailani and her death immediately following. I had always imagined writing a book about my hardships, though I thought it would be about my lifelong journey of fighting with eating disorders and body image. There was never a time when I thought I would be joining the group of grieving parents in the death of a child.

My intention for writing this book has three parts. The first is to honour and keep the memory of my beautiful daughter Kailani alive. Shortly after her birth and death, I developed this fear that her memory would be forgotten, and there was no way I would allow that to happen.

Second, I hope that through my own experience of loss and navigating through grief, I might be able to assist others in their journey. There are many layers to grief and, to be honest, we often do not immediately identify, recognize, or realize these layers until we live through such heartache. By recognizing and talking about them, I hope to bring an awareness to others about the reality of a grieving parent and share methods I have used to maintain my sanity through it all and focus on creating a new life where grief and joy coexist. In creating awareness of the reality of grief following the loss of a baby, I also explore societal expectations and responses to grief and how we can modify this, moving forward, to better support, understand, and demonstrate compassion and acceptance to those who are grieving.

Lastly, I want to thank all the mothers, fathers, grandparents, and other family members who have shared the names of their angels to be honoured in these pages. Though their lives were fleeting, the memory of them lives on. No matter how short, their lives have changed us to our core, are forever loved, and never forgotten. This book is to honour each and every baby that ever existed. Your lives matter. The experience of each grieving parent, grandparent, and family member matters.

Now, I do not claim to be some guru who has all the answers to grief following the death of a baby. Having experienced many hardships and trauma, I believe my experiences have allowed me to cultivate a level of resilience where I've been able to adopt a way to not only survive following the death of my daughter, but also to thrive. Through sharing our experiences, I truly feel we can help support, inspire, and empower others in their journey while also helping to create awareness about pregnancy and infant loss and eliminating the stigma that exists within our society.

FOR MY MOMMY AND DADDY
By Kathy Randall

I'm so sorry I had to go,
Your world was not for me to know.

My heart was heavy and filled with sorrow,
Sadness filled me with our loss of tomorrow.

I'm so sorry I had to go,
For reasons unexplained we may never know.

The love we shared will last forever,
Until the day we are again together.

Suddenly I was lifted as if by grace,
Over the Rainbow Bridge, oh what a place.

From there I'll watch over the two of you below,
I'm so sorry I had to go.

Love Forever and Always,
Kailani Mary Randall

THIRTY-ONE WEEKS
AND TWO DAYS PREGNANT

July 21, 2020 – Just a typical Tuesday morning, no different than the week prior. We were heading to Alberta for an ultrasound appointment the next morning. We woke up at seven, so we could get on the road for nine. We figured we would get a relatively early start. With the pelvic and rib pain I had been experiencing for the past few weeks, we anticipated that what would typically be a five-hour trip would end up being a full day. Matt figured that I would need lots of breaks, if not for the pain and discomfort, then to pee. What we didn't anticipate was that this day marked the start of a week that would change our lives and souls forever.

Though it was just another Tuesday morning, things were a little bit different than the weeks and days prior. I woke up, rocked my way to the side of the bed, and sat there for a moment. This had become my everyday routine, starting sometime during the second trimester.

When a baby is growing inside of you, there is no space for oxygen, food, urine, or anything. Not only that, a few weeks before, I had received a diagnosis of polyhydramnios, which translates to having too much amniotic fluid. I am quite certain that any and all abdominal muscles I may have had prior to my pregnancy packed up and left. Any type of mobilization or turning became my daily form of exercise.

1

Turning in bed and getting out of bed became one of the most challenging tasks in my day. I am not even joking. Therefore, once seated at the side of the bed, I would take a moment to catch my breath, get my swollen feet under me, and then proceed to the bathroom for the third or fourth pee since midnight.

That morning, however, something was different. Something happened between me sitting and actually getting to the bathroom. When I stood, I immediately felt a gush of fluid. Now, I had been experiencing small amounts of leakage over the past few weeks, though it was nothing like this. I mean, it was quite a bit of fluid, but I would not have classified this sensation as my water breaking. I must admit, however, that it was more fluid than what I had been passing the previous week.

I didn't really think much of it and figured it was likely due to me having slept for more than two hours straight without getting up for a bathroom break. I was so grateful to have slept for that stretch of time.

I went and cleaned myself up, got dressed, and started to pack. To be on the safe side, I'd decided I better use two panty liners, as I would not have quick access to a bathroom once we were on the road.

Within thirty minutes, I felt another gush of fluid. I started the internal self-talk process and began reasoning with myself. *It is fine. I'm just moving around lots. I am going for a medical follow-up, and I can tell them when I get there. It is no big deal.* However, at my thirty-week follow-up with my maternity doctor, I was told that if I experienced an increase in fluid leakage, I would need to call her immediately and go to the hospital. This was because one of the possible complications of polyhydramnios is preterm rupture of membranes and possibly preterm labour.

Now, although I knew that those were possibilities, I truly thought all was fine and dandy. I mean, really, I just wanted to get to Calgary so I could receive an ultrasound and hopefully find out why I had the polyhydramnios to begin with. I mean, so what if I now have to use a couple extra pads?

The week prior, I might have used two panty liners in a day; however, by the time we loaded up the truck and hit the road to Calgary, I had already gone through five that morning. Not only that, the amount of fluid was enough to saturate the liners, my underwear, and my pants on two occasions. All within a two-hour window. Like I said, this Tuesday morning was slightly different.

Then just before I was about to put my shoes on to leave, I had this internal voice tell me that I needed to head back to my room and grab my affirmation cards. I don't typically pull affirmation cards before I leave on a trip, though a voice inside my head said that I need to pull *three* cards and ask the universe what specifically I need to focus on over the next couple days. I am sure you might be thinking I am crazy at this point, though over the past year, I had been working on practising daily gratitude and affirmations to support my mindset. So just stay with me. My cards were as follows:

1. No Judgment—I tell my inner critic to take a vacation. As it leaves, I begin to enjoy the joy of simply being and release myself from any and all judgment.

2. Peacefulness—My heart is peaceful, tranquil, and untroubled. I choose to spend my time here. Any person, thought, or event that brings chaos or drama is not invited. My heart is special, and I am going to keep it in peacefulness, so we can all enjoy it.

3. Positive Thinking—My mind is a garden, and I choose to water the good thoughts and weed out the bad. I place forgiveness and empathy seeds in my garden and take a lawnmower to jealousy and resentment. I am one badass mind gardener.

Of course, I automatically had assumed this had to do with the trip ahead of us or maybe the leakage I was experiencing. I didn't think too much about it at that time. Though I did take pictures of the cards for reference, then proceeded to get my shoes on. We managed to get on the road at 8:43 a.m.

3

Naturally, my mom wanted me to let her know we were leaving, so I gave her a call. I told her about the events that had occurred that morning, and she wanted me to call the doctor immediately to let them know what had happened. My mom, like so many moms out there, is what I like to call a worrywart. (You know it's true, Mom, and I love you for it!)

After speaking with her, I called the clinic and asked the receptionist to relay a message to my doctor. I reassured her it was not urgent and explained the situation. Because I work very closely with everyone at the clinic, they knew how to reach me if needed. At 9:08 a.m., the maternity physician on-call contacted me and asked, "Where are you?" I relayed to her that I was on my way to Calgary and that we had just left.

She clarified, "No, where specifically on the road are you?"

My immediate thought was, *Well, shit just got serious.* My second thought, *Matt was totally right; this was going to be a twelve-hour trip.*

We were about halfway to the next town. She gave me instructions to go directly to the hospital. She told me that she would call me right back with further direction, as she wanted to speak with the specialist at the hospital we were headed to. At 9:11 a.m., three minutes after our initial conversation, she called and told me to report directly to the maternity unit on the second floor of the hospital. No need to register or go through the emergency room. Just get to the unit, and they would have everything ready for me.

I cannot specifically remember the last thing she said to me, though it was something along the lines of "All the best and be sure to keep me up to date."

I didn't think that this was really anything to be concerned about or that I would have much to update her on. I truly had every intention of just getting to Calgary and letting them know what had happened when I got there. I should have known better, though. That lack of concern would soon change.

PPROM? WELL SHIT

When we got to the hospital and I stepped out of the truck, another gush of fluid immediately came shooting out of me. We walked through the front doors to be greeted by two ladies who were screening individuals for COVID-19. We sanitized our hands and donned our masks. We were asked if we needed directions to the second floor, though I was familiar with the hospital, having worked here in the past. We headed to the elevators and made our way up to the second floor.

We walked past the surgical reception area to a set of locked double doors and rang the bell. A nurse scanned her key card, and the doors opened. We walked through the doors and were greeted by a couple of nurses and a unit clerk; they had been expecting us. They had already received copies of all my information and registered me in the system. Matt and I were escorted to a private room.

I sat on the bed, and immediately the nurse began connecting me to the fetal non-stress test (NST) machine, a test I had received the day prior in our hometown. For those not familiar, this machine allows practitioners to monitor the baby's heart rate and movement, and measure contractions.

The NST did not show anything of concern. The baby's heart rate fluctuated between 120–150 beats per minute, which was normal. I was not experiencing any contractions during this time and quite enjoyed hearing our baby move around inside the womb. I had discovered, during the NST done the previous day, that our little angel liked to move around quite a bit. However, it wasn't very often that I could feel the baby moving. This was due to having too much amniotic fluid present.

Matt sat in the chair toward the foot of the bed while I remained hooked up to the NST. I told him he should begin taking pictures to start documenting our journey. I figured it was important to capture each step of the process so that one day we would be able to share everything with our child. Also, just a little side note, if you haven't caught on yet, we did not know if we were having a girl or a boy at this time.

As we waited for the specialist, Matt and I agreed that we shouldn't worry our parents at that point. Especially my mom. Knowing her, she would have packed a bag, drove to the hospital, and made some new record time. To be honest, while we were on route to the hospital, Matt and I joked that if we had told her where we were headed, she would have beat us there. For that reason, we figured it was best just to wait and see what was happening before sharing any type of details with our parents.

After about twenty minutes of monitoring, the specialist came in and started asking some questions. He had read through my reports and understood that I was diagnosed with polyhydramnios. I confirmed and shared with him that due to the diagnosis, I was told I would require additional follow-up, which was why we were on our way to Calgary that day.

He started asking me more detailed questions about the amount of fluid that had come out of me that morning. As I was wearing liners and it was soaking through my underwear and pants, it was difficult to give him an actual measured amount. He listened and made mental notes of everything I shared. He then went on to explain what the next steps were.

The primary concern at this point was whether or not the fluid I was leaking was amniotic. If it was, this would mean that I had experienced preterm premature rupture of membranes (PPROM). If this were the case, I would immediately need to be transferred to a larger site that could support a preterm delivery and baby. The doctor relayed that in these types of situations, labour could occur right away, or it could be days or even weeks before anything happened. However, there was no way to know for sure, so they wanted to get me to a centre that could support me and our baby, should I deliver at thirty-one weeks.

Next came the swabbing to test the fluid. I was familiar with this process, as I'd had the same procedure done when I told my maternity doctor about my fluid leakage a few weeks prior. When testing for amniotic fluid, they use a specific swab. If the fluid is amniotic, the swab tip changes colour to blue. Immediately, my swab changed colour. Even the doctor commented on how dark the swab went, as it almost looked black instead of blue. I wasn't able to maintain my indoor voice at that point. Next thing I heard myself saying was, "Well shit." Dr. H looked at me and simply nodded in agreement.

He took the sample to the lab to view it under the microscope. He returned shortly after and told us that he has confirmed what he suspected; the fluid was amniotic in nature and my membranes had ruptured. He said that their next step would be to arrange transfer to a larger hospital.

Typically, this would mean a transfer to a site out in Vancouver, British Columbia. However, he said they would see if they could arrange a transfer to Calgary. I mean, it was closer for Matt to drive, plus we had a bunch of family there, and I mean, they were already expecting us. It would definitely be preferable. The staff shared that, most often, clients were not accepted from out of province, and Vancouver might be our only option. However, they were willing to make the effort and started making the necessary phone calls and arrangements.

No specific timeline was set for me to be transferred, though Dr. H relayed that it would be sometime that afternoon. Due to the potential risk and complications that could arise, they would not allow me to travel by vehicle, and I would need to be flown. Matt began making phone calls to our parents.

. . .

7

As the team coordinated my transfer, I had a couple of nurses come in to take my vital signs and administer some medications. The first medication was an injection of steroids to help develop the baby's lungs more rapidly, in case of early delivery. I received one dose at 12 p.m. and would receive a second dose in twenty-four hours. They also hooked me up to an intravenous line with antibiotics. Due to my ruptured membranes, I was at an increased risk for infection.

Then out of nowhere, I started receiving visitors. First, my stepmom came in, as she was working in the recovery unit. We gave her a quick update to relay to my dad. I had called him prior to her stopping in, though I had to cut the call short as a lab technician came to draw some blood.

Next, my stepsister popped in, who happens to work on the floor above. It looked like she had been crying, and she kept her distance. Lastly, one of my maternity doctors made a surprise appearance and came to check in on me. I was shocked to see her there, as she was the doctor scheduled to be working back home in our maternity clinic that morning. She wished me luck and reminded me to obtain copies of everything prior to leaving Calgary and coming home.

Once things settled down, I immediately grabbed my phone and started making phone calls. I needed to cancel my ultrasound and the hotel, and start preparing for a trip to Vancouver. Then it hit me. *I need to prepare for the arrival of our baby!*

I didn't pack the car seat, no blankets, no clothing, nothing. I was supposed to be getting an ultrasound. I was supposed to be gone for two days and returning home, very much pregnant. Once home, I had plans of putting the final touches together in the nursery. Then I had another thought. *The nursery is not complete.* I am sure if someone would have checked my blood pressure during this time, it would have been sky high. I mean, I had not thought about the possibility of our baby arriving early. Things were happening all so quickly. I couldn't think, my heart started racing, breathing became difficult, and my muscles tightened.

Fortunately, Matt was able to ground me and reassured me that we would work it all out in the end. We always do. Also, there was no way that a baby born at thirty-one weeks would be coming home anytime soon. Rest assured, we had time.

. . .

Before I knew it, two paramedics arrived at the door, wearing respirators. I was told that Calgary had accepted me, which surprised the physician and the nurses. Unfortunately, they would not allow Matt to fly with me, and he would have to meet me there. Fortunately, Calgary is much closer than Vancouver, so he only had a four-hour drive ahead of him versus ten hours.

In all the chaos, I can remember thinking to myself, *It's a good thing I pack my underwear as though I might poop myself multiple times per day.* My anticipatory two-day trip required at least five pairs of undies. *Five pairs—that should get me through*, I figured. *That is a plus.*

The paramedics took my vital signs and offered me some Gravol for the trip. Initially, I declined, as Gravol makes me feel nauseous. However, the paramedic convinced me that sitting backwards in the ambulance and in an airplane tends to make people feel rather unwell. So, I finally agreed to a half dose. I admit, I might be a bit stubborn.

I went pee one last time before settling onto the stretcher and giving Matt a kiss goodbye. He then grabbed the items we had brought in with us and left the unit to get back on the road. They wheeled me down the hallway, past the nursing stations, to the elevator. As we passed the nurses, they wished me luck.

For some reason, sitting on that stretcher and being wheeled off the unit with the nurses watching me was like being naked on a stage in front of thousands of people. Why did this feel so uncomfortable? In that moment, I found myself at a loss for words. My body began to tense up again. I could feel a familiar heaviness dropping onto my shoulders.

What awaits me in Calgary? Why does the nurses' farewell have such a darkness to it? Or maybe I am making it up in my head. Do they know something I don't? How will all this unfold?

CHECKING
EMOTIONAL BAGGAGE

The ambulance ride to the airport was uneventful. I had never been in the back of an ambulance before; another first to add to my list. While the ambulance attendant completed some paperwork, I simply observed. Everything in the ambulance had its place. It was clean and everything was secured.

The windows out the back of the ambulance were covered to blur the view. Only the top quarter of the window remained clear, and I watched the blue sky and clouds as we made our way to the airport. *What a beautiful day*, I thought.

The drive was short, only about fifteen minutes. However, I could not get comfortable. I was constantly trying to shuffle myself on the stretcher to alleviate the discomfort. The pain in my pelvis and ribs was constant now, and I wanted nothing more than to unstrap myself and move around. In the truck, I at least had the ability to shift from side to side and move the seat. Plus, I had the heat option for my back. Does the stretcher offer these options?

When we arrived at the airport, the aircraft had landed, and the ground crew was preparing for our departure. One of the attendants from the plane hopped into the ambulance with us. He received handover from the ambulance attendant and then proceeded to explain the process for loading me into the plane. Should I need anything during the flight, I would need to call out, wave my arms, do whatever I needed to do to get their attention. As I would be in the rear of the plane, facing backwards, I would need to get creative to flag down the crew. When they say holler, they meant it. In a tiny plane like that, all you are left with is the roaring sound of the engines and the noise of your mind.

As the crew disassembled the loading ramp and secured it to the back of the plane, my mind started to wander. The forty-five-minute flight gave me time to reflect on my pregnancy. *Was there a clue or did I miss something during my pregnancy that led to this? Was it my first trimester? My second trimester? Maybe I overdid it? Was it something I did? Should I be more concerned with my diagnosis of too much amniotic fluid?* The wave of thoughts hit hard, and I spaced out.

. . .

About eight months prior to getting pregnant, I decided to have my intrauterine device (IUD) removed. I told Matt from the start of our relationship that I wanted children. However, part of me knew that even if I didn't have children, I would be okay with that too. I figured that if it was meant to be, it was meant to be. I had my IUD removed and had zero expectations. We would just see what life had in store for us and accept whatever came our way.

To be completely honest, part of me didn't think I would actually get pregnant. In a previous relationship, I tried for about three years without any luck. When we broke up, he and his girlfriend were pregnant within a couple of months. I just assumed that I couldn't have children.

The weekend after my birthday in January 2020 was when we discovered we were pregnant. In December, I noticed that my energy levels started to deplete. Exercising became a non-priority, primarily because I couldn't find the energy. I really wanted nothing more than to have regular naps throughout the day. Then when I was late with my period in January, I started to wonder.

On January 26, 2020, I peed on a stick. It confirmed what both Matt and I had suspected. I mean, the symptoms I was experiencing at that time were classic pregnancy symptoms. Regardless, reading that "Pregnant +3" was a bit of a shock. I had always said that if I didn't get pregnant before thirty, I would not have children. Go figure. I managed to conceive just before my thirtieth birthday. The crazy thing, I can recall telling Matt back in December that he should consider booking an appointment for the all juice and no seed procedure, since I was coming up on the big three zero. Funny how life happens.

. . .

During my first trimester, I experienced all the typical pregnancy symptoms. Nausea, vomiting, tender breasts, exhaustion, the works. Who knew that being pregnant was so incredibly exhausting? I tried getting back into my exercise routine and would become completely out of breath, to the point of feeling like passing out within five minutes. How on Earth do some of these women do it!? I didn't even have a baby bump yet, and I swear gravity had me floored one hundred percent of the time.

The smell of meat cooking and the texture of it was something that absolutely disgusted me. All I wanted to eat all day, every day, was watermelon and cantaloupe. My diet during the first trimester became primarily vegetarian. I also found a new obsession with sour candies. More specifically, sour keys and Sour Patch Kids. Toward the end of the first trimester, I also fell in love with ice cream again, something I have always loved, although it often makes me sick.

My potassium levels were slightly elevated, and my sodium levels were down. However, no treatments were required at that time. I simply was more mindful of what I was putting in my body. I eliminated bananas and started implementing some more salt.

. . .

Work was busier than ever, due to COVID-19. There were new processes, procedures, and policies being implemented throughout the hospital. Things were stressful, and I didn't really think too much about how that stress might be affecting me and my baby. I mean, everyone was stressed out. Though, I had always been the type of person that thrives off stress and enjoys an overflowing plate.

My family often jokes about how I am addicted to stress, which is a lie. I just like to remain busy all of the time. To keep myself busy, I decided to cram a two-year diploma program into a year, only to overlap it with a full-time master's degree, and then accepted a full-time position of clinical operations manager. I've always been one to load or overload my plate. That was just my life and how I operate. I enjoy pushing myself and reaching new limits. Part of this mindset I cultivated from a quote by Fred DeVito, "If it doesn't challenge you, it doesn't change you." This is a quote I've applied to almost every aspect of my life. It actually hangs in my office and is something that has helped push me forward in the writing of this book.

• • •

I continued to work from the hospital during my first trimester and most of my second, in an effort to support staff and coworkers. Though I no longer work directly with clients and families in my position, I felt it important that the team felt supported by leadership members and that I remain available and accessible on-site.

It was stressful, and there was always the thought of becoming sick in the back of my mind; however, I felt that role modelling specific behaviours and being accessible to the team was essential during these really challenging times and trumped everything else. My family, of course, did not agree with my approach. When I finally told my work family at the beginning of the second trimester that I was expecting, I had a couple of individuals approach me and request that I remain home because they, too, were concerned about me and the baby's wellness. As you've likely caught on by now, I am one stubborn woman and filed these requests under future considerations.

. . .

During the second trimester, I started to regain my energy levels. I definitely needed this, as we had been approved a mortgage for our very first home. It was like all the cards were falling into place. We discovered we were pregnant and the home we had been looking at since October 2019 was going to be ours come April 2020. I was convinced that the universe was in alignment for us.

With my new-found energy, I was able to help with painting, packing, and moving. Of course, keeping it to the lighter items and trying not to overdo it. Matt and my family were on my case constantly and observing my every move, as I was determined to not let my pregnancy limit my capacity to help in any way.

My appetite returned and I was back to eating regular meals. The nausea and vomiting had pretty much stopped, with a few exceptions here and there. I can remember getting ready for work one morning and heading into town. I ended up having to pull over quickly to eliminate breakfast. And yes, six months later, I can still tell you exactly what I had that morning. My cousin happened to be on her way to work that morning as well and saw me pull over. She sent me a message to check in on me. I assured her all was well and that the baby did not agree with my breakfast selection.

My potassium levels had gone back to normal; however, my sodium continued to drop. Due to the ongoing electrolyte imbalance, one of my maternity doctors ordered me to go in for biweekly blood work. We continued to monitor my levels and my sodium continued to deplete. At that point, one of my maternity doctors prescribed sodium chloride. I was hopeful that this would help with the intense headaches and muscle spasms I had started experiencing.

I was experiencing headaches more and more frequently, which is not something new for me. I've suffered from migraines and tension headaches for the past ten years. However, there were days where I was unable to do anything except lie on the couch. Some days the only thing that provided any relief was lying with an acupressure pillow against the back of my head and neck. I refused to take any medication, as I didn't want to place our baby at risk. As one of the symptoms of low sodium can be headaches, I assumed this was the cause and continued to hold onto hope that things would improve with the new medication.

Other than the low sodium, headaches, and muscle spasms, the second trimester was where it was at. I felt strong. I felt healthy. My appointments went smoothly. I had people tell me I didn't even look like I was pregnant for the first part of the second trimester. All was going well. Then, I started to experience some pelvic pain around the twenty-week mark. Fortunately, I was able to schedule an appointment to see a physiotherapist that specializes in maternal health.

Around week twenty-one, I started to notice my body shifting. I literally woke up one morning to a very large baby bump. I literally grew overnight. No joke. I saw my brother three days before I grew my bump, and when he saw me, his jaw hit the ground. Not only was I now visibly pregnant, I was *extremely* pregnant. With this shift came relief in my pelvis, though I was not about to cancel my physiotherapy appointment.

When I went to see the physiotherapist, I discovered that my pain was due to having a retrospective uterus. Apparently, my uterus sits differently in my pelvis, which meant the baby had been growing in my pelvis for the first little while. Then around month five, the baby typically wiggles their way out of the pelvic area so they have more room to grow; hence, why I felt such relief when I woke up to a huge baby bump.

Once the baby shifted, my body continued to experience some more changes. I started experiencing late-stage pregnancy symptoms early on. I became extremely short of breath with even the smallest motions. My legs ballooned overnight. One day I was wearing my size medium Fabletics tights; the next day, I couldn't get them past my calves.

I started wearing compression stockings, though the stockings would cut into my legs. My doctor ended up putting me on water pills to help eliminate some of the fluid. Over a period of about three weeks, things improved slightly. However, I ended up discontinuing the pills as I found my blood pressure was becoming affected and I was often dizzy.

Therefore, my legs remained swollen. Most of my clothes no longer fit because I couldn't get anything over my legs. The dresses that I had kept out, thinking I could wear them during pregnancy, were a no go. They fit my stomach, though I had not thought about how much my boobs would grow. Why hello there, you voluptuous beauties (definitely a plus side for those of us that don't have these bad boys).

Ordering clothing online was a bit of a challenge. Due to the delays in delivery time from the pandemic, I found that I would order an item, and by the time it arrived, it didn't fit due to my rapid growth. Sweatpants and baggy T-shirts for the win!

As the weeks progressed, the pain and discomfort increased. Even the smallest amount of activity would have me huffing and puffing as though I just ran a marathon. Regardless, I pushed myself to go for a walk every day, hoping that this would help maintain my cardiovascular capacity—the little bit that I had left. Plus, I felt bad for Gibson (our black lab) because throwing his ball and playing with him became more and more challenging. Going for a walk was good for both of us, and it became part of our daily routine.

Then one morning, shortly after I started my workday, I found myself having a conversation with a co-worker. She shared her experiences of working while pregnant. During her first pregnancy, she had worked in a high-stress position and pushed herself, not taking into consideration the effect it might have on her son. When he arrived, he was very colicky and remained this way for his first year. During her second pregnancy, she took a different approach and was able to remain calmer and stress-free. She said her daughter was the complete opposite of her son, and she truly feels that her children were affected by her work environments during her pregnancies. After this conversation, I decided I needed to shift my priorities. I needed to start really focusing on me and our baby. It was time to start working from home.

. . .

At week twenty-six, I went for a regular follow-up with my doctor. She measured my stomach, which, unsurprisingly, was considerably larger than what would have been expected for how far along I was. She ordered another ultrasound so we could obtain measurements of the baby. In the back of my mind, I thought, *Maybe I am carrying twins?* That seemed much more ideal versus the possibility of growing a miniature giant and having to push that out of me. No thank you.

During this visit, I shared with her that I had been experiencing some discharge. She completed an internal exam and tested for amniotic fluid. The swab came back negative and she confirmed this in the lab. Other than that, everything else was going normal; or at least that was what I thought, because I didn't know any different. Before I left, she told me should anything change—specifically if I experienced an increase in discharge, a change in colour, odour, etc.—that I needed to come to the hospital immediately. Mental note made.

. . .

My previous ultrasounds did not reveal anything of concern, based on the reports. I had my initial ultrasound at eight weeks, then a second at twenty-one weeks. At the twenty-one-week scan, we couldn't complete the assessment due to the baby's position. Therefore, I was scheduled to go back in two weeks, in hopes that the baby's position had changed. Turns out, this baby was stubborn like their momma. As in the previous images, the babe was facing backwards, hands covering up the face or they had their thumb in their mouth. Therefore, a clear picture of our baby's face was not obtained, as per the ultrasound technician. Strangely, the report completed and uploaded in my file suggested a different story, as the radiologist indicated, "Images of the fetal nose and lips are obtained and are unremarkable."

Following my twenty-six-week follow-up, another ultrasound was scheduled to determine if I was growing a miniature giant in me. The appointment I received was initially set for the end of July. I figured that was a bit far out and that this should be a priority, so I called the regional hospital to see about getting an appointment sooner. The soonest they could schedule me in was for July 15, 2020. I figured four weeks from my appointment was much better than the initial six. In my mind, I thought it should have been investigated and made a priority. However, babies and maternal health are not my area of expertise, so I just assumed that all was well and kept my thoughts to myself.

At about week twenty-nine, I started to experience excruciating pelvic pain. I can't even find the words to describe what this was like. I've always considered myself to have a high pain tolerance and I could not place a pain score to this. As a nurse, I would tell clients that a pain of one to three out of ten is something one might consider manageable and does not affect sleeping patterns. Pain scored at a four to six is something that wakes you from a sleep. Anything above a six means you cannot fall asleep.

The pain I had in my pelvis was so intense that I spent seventy-two consecutive hours awake and could not stop moving. I refused to take any type of medications. One position that relieved my pain was if I sat on the floor with my feet together and knees bent out. I tried stacking pillows to rest my head on to get some sleep; it didn't work. Trying to lie down was extremely painful. Lying down for another ultrasound was not something I was looking forward to. This could not possibly be how I was going to spend the remainder of my pregnancy. I would lose my mind.

When I went in for my ultrasound at thirty weeks, I struggled to lie on the table. My life became constant pain. There was a stabbing pain, combined with an intense ache and burning fire in my pelvis and lower back. I was convinced that I had a rib in my right side that was broken and puncturing a lung. I tried to sit still as best as I could, though I wanted nothing more than to reposition onto my side or stand. Because this ultrasound was to assess the growth of our baby, it was a little bit longer than my previous appointments. I could tell the ultrasound tech felt bad and was a bit frustrated with all my movement; I couldn't help myself.

The day after my ultrasound, I received a phone call from my maternity doctor. She said that the ultrasound confirmed that I had too much amniotic fluid and that she had consulted with a specialist out of the regional hospital, an hour away. I would require additional lab work, twice-weekly monitoring at the hospital, as well as additional imaging out of province to investigate the cause of the additional amniotic fluid. Great . . . what does that mean?

Of course, my mind started to really think. *Way to go LaCara! Why not get pregnant for my first time during a pandemic? The nurse who offers prenatal classes in our town is on maternity leave, so that resource is not available. To boot, due to COVID-19, all the usual resources have been placed on hold. Follow-ups and visits have been decreased to limit exposure and are being done remotely over the telephone. Furthermore, Matt has not been able to attend appointments with me. He is out of the loop and excluded in some ways. Plus, we've purchased a new home and are working to complete renovations before our due date of September 20, 2020. Hell, how about we add on polyhydramnios? I mean, if anyone can handle this shit, it is us. We got this. Totally. Seriously, LaCara. I know you like stress, but you need to chill and stop being an overachiever.*

When I received this news, I was sitting at the kitchen table. Matt was at work, and I was alone. After hanging up the phone, I started to cry. I mean, being pregnant through a pandemic is an interesting experience, especially for a first-time mom like myself. Now add to my stress by diagnosing me with polyhydramnios and needing to explore the cause. I had no clue what this meant. So, of course, I did what I was trained to do. Time to research.

I wasn't familiar with this condition and needed to look it up. Polyhydramnios occurs in approximately one to two percent of all pregnancies, and approximately fifty percent of these cases have a known cause. With this diagnosis comes a list of potential complications, including premature birth, premature rupture of membranes, placental abruption, umbilical cord prolapses, heavy bleeding, and stillbirth. I have always held the belief that knowledge is power. However, in this case, knowing the increased risks associated with my pregnancy did not help my anxious mind. Furthermore, we didn't yet know the cause of my polyhydramnios. My mind immediately started going through the possible causes and the complications that accompanied each of them.

Matt is always my voice of reason, and he wasn't there to calm me down. I didn't want to call him at work, so I called my mom instead. I am pretty sure my stepdad texted Matt and told him to call me. I do not typically get phone calls from Matt during his workday, though on this day, I did. Honestly, I needed it as my mind was wandering and going down some deep, dark holes.

"It happens in one to two percent of pregnancies. This means that there are professionals that can manage this, and all will be okay. This is why we are going for more testing, and a specialist has been consulted. Trust that it will all work out, my love," Matt reassured me. My breathing and heart rate began to slow.

Thank God for Matt and his ability to calm me. I often joke that he is my calming goat, like Lupe from the children's movie *Ferdinand*. You would think that as a nurse, I could reason with myself. Yeah, no. Definitely not. I am pretty sure all doctors and nurses will say that we make the worst patients. To be honest, I have to agree.

I cannot speak for all healthcare professionals, though I am one who either downplays the reality of a situation or assumes the worst-case scenario. There is no in between or rationalizing. At that point, I began feeling overwhelmed with how the day was panning out. I tried to remain optimistic that good things were on the horizon, though, in hindsight, I should have been very concerned.

• • •

Before I knew it, we were descending to land. Anyone who has travelled to Alberta via air knows that it is windy. The turbulence wasn't horrible that day, though the smaller the plane, the more turbulence you feel. This plane was tiny.

After touching down, it felt like we had driven around the airport for a good ten or fifteen minutes. I was almost convinced they were driving along a runway from the airport to the hospital. I was really hoping that this was the case because, at this point, I needed to pee.

It took the pilots and the medical team a while to get everything sorted once we came to a stop. There were ramps and cables that needed to be hooked up in order to unload me from the plane. I was not allowed to walk off the plane, so they had to unload the stretcher using some electronic contraption. The Alberta ambulance crew arrived right on time and assisted the flight crew with unloading. I made the request for a bathroom break, knowing that there was a twenty-minute ride ahead. Plus, who knew what the traffic situation would look like.

I had asked one of the crew members from the plane if there was a bathroom I might be able to use. I specified "a facility restroom" as they previously told me that they had bedpans for use if I had the urge. That was a no go for me; I would continue to hold.

As the team completed the handover, the ambulance attendants were told that they might get brownie points with me if they allowed me to use the restroom before loading me into the ambulance. I am so very grateful that the airport crew approved me to use their facilities. They, of course, wanted to know if I was sick and had COVID-19. They were reassured that I was totally fine and was simply an uncomfortable pregnant lady who really needed to pee.

Go figure, they would not allow me to walk into the building and to the bathroom. I was rolled in on the stretcher. Seeing that bathroom door was such relief. Walking into the stall, I was all like, *Why hello, gorgeous. My throne awaits me.* Thank you again to those kind ambulance attendants for allowing me to use the restroom. Truth be told, as much as I say I would have held it, there is no such thing as holding it when you are pregnant.

THE LABYRINTH
OF HEALTHCARE

It was approximately four in the evening when they loaded me into the ambulance and we started on our way. We went through the same process that I had gone through just an hour before; the same set of questions, routine vital signs, and paperwork. Most people get frustrated with this process and how healthcare professionals ask the same questions over and over again, though I've come to appreciate it to a certain extent.

So many things get lost in translation. Bits and pieces of information tend to get forgotten or left out when passed from one person to the next. Ensuring they had all the information was key for me and our baby to receive the care we needed. For that reason, I took on the mindset of "ask away." The questions didn't take much time and, really, what else was I going to do?

As I anticipated, it was about a twenty-minute ride to Foothills Hospital. I am grateful that I did not have to drive, as I have never been one for city traffic. Whenever Matt and I go on road trips, Matt is the one who takes the wheel. In part, this is due to me having zero sense of direction. Additionally, Matt doesn't mind driving, where I am not overly keen on driving long distances. Also, Matt previously lived in Calgary, so he is familiar with how to get around and where everything is located. I, on the other hand, rely heavily on google maps. Furthermore, I cannot stand rush hour, lineups, and idiotic drivers. I mean, to be honest, idiots are everywhere; there are just more of them in the larger cities.

As we got closer to our destination, I could see parts of the hospital, and our speed began to slow. The set-up at Foothills was different from what I have experienced at other hospitals. They had an ambulance bay where we parked that had a separate entrance into the building. This meant we didn't have to go through the emergency room, unlike the smaller sites I was familiar with back home.

The two attendants unloaded me from the vehicle, and we found a small opening between two ambulances to squeeze past and make our way to the entrance. Once we went through the doors, I was amazed at how many individuals were waiting in the hallway. There were ambulance attendants and police officers talking, with a couple of patients strapped to stretchers, all pushed up along the wall.

Everyone seemed to know one another. One of the individuals in the hallway told one of the attendants pushing me that he needed to talk to him. He seemed ready to have the conversation in that moment, though the attendant pushing me said he would catch him on his way back. He told the group that we were heading upstairs.

When I say group, I mean there were approximately twenty people waiting in this hallway. That familiar and yet uncomfortable feeling crept up on me as the ambulance attendants and police officers cleared a pathway and moved up against the walls, allowing us to pass through. As we made our way past, everyone took their turn glancing our way. I am sure they were wondering why a young pregnant lady who was not visibly distressed was being wheeled in on a stretcher.

We stopped at the elevators and took the service elevator up to the fifth floor. They dropped me off at the labour and delivery triage unit at approximately 5 p.m. I didn't stay in this unit for long, although I met a couple of physicians and nurses during my time there. I came to learn that many of the nurses that work on this unit actually work in the other maternity units as well.

Immediately upon admission, I was hooked up to the NST machine. The nurse struggled to find the baby's heartbeat on the machine due to all the fluid I was carrying. We could hear it faintly, though the machine wasn't picking it up enough to record it on paper. Finally, she found the sweet spot.

I remained hooked to the machine for approximately half an hour. No changes were noted from when I had been hooked up earlier that day. The staff didn't know that, though I was watching my numbers. My vitals remained stable, I didn't have any contractions, and the baby's heartbeat continued to fluctuate between 120–150 beats per minute. I could hear our baby moving around lots, though I couldn't actually feel it. I typically only felt movement in the evenings between 8 and 10. It was usually just a kick or two to the rib cage or my bladder. Feeling our baby move around was always comforting. Oh, our sweet little angel, how I couldn't wait to meet you.

There really was nothing to do during my time on this unit, other than sit and wait. One of the nurses came and asked me if I would prefer a private room for an additional cost of $110 per day. I really didn't see the point in that, as the nurse told me that Matt would *not* be able to remain in the hospital with me. That would have meant we were paying for a hotel and a hospital room. No, thank you; especially if this was going to be a long, drawn-out stay.

Plus, my thinking was that due to COVID-19, they would likely try to spread out clients in hospital rooms. I mean, this was our approach back home. So really, maybe there was the possibility that I would end up getting the room to myself. Even if I didn't, it might be nice to make a new pregnant friend.

. . .

I received a message from Matt, who was approximately an hour and a half from the city. He put me to work and asked that I look up the parking situation at the hospital. I was very grateful that parking fees were not outrageous. I mean, there was the possibility that I might end up staying in this hospital until I reached full-term. Did I forget to mention that? Yeah, this place might end up being my home away from home. My fingers and toes were crossed that this would not be the case.

There appeared to be ample parking available, and I figured this was due to COVID-19 and visitor restrictions. Once Matt arrived, he actually discovered that there was no cost for parking. I assumed the parking meters were closed due to COVID-19 and these being an additional way for transmission of the virus. Either way, thank you, Alberta Health Services.

By the time Matt arrived, I had been transferred to the antepartum unit on the fourth floor. It was just after 7 p.m. when he arrived. Bonus part, he brought food! I was so hungry. The nurse had told me she called down to the kitchen a couple of times, though I figured I must have missed the window for dinner when I was admitted. I can't even remember what I ate for breakfast that morning or if I even ate. I did eat half of a tuna sandwich when we were in Cranbrook. To be honest, I wasn't looking forward to hospital food, so I was very grateful and welcomed the food Matt was carrying in that bag.

That grilled chicken clubhouse from Boston Pizza was almost orgasmic. I cannot remember the last time I had one of those, but diggity dang it was delicious. Of course, as I was shovelling my face full of food, someone from the kitchen came up with a tray. I might have read her expression wrong, though I am convinced that she gave me a look of disgust. I imagine she was thinking something like, "Seriously, you're eating that, and you're going to eat this meal I just brought you?" *Uh, thank you, but I am quite satisfied with this here and will have to pass on what you just brought me. Though I will keep that fruit cup and orange juice for later.*

. . .

At 7:30 p.m., shift change took place. My new nurse came in and introduced herself. She hooked me up to the NST again and took my vitals. She said that I would receive an ultrasound the next morning, though there wasn't a specific time. They would just pop down and grab me. She asked if Matt would be staying with me. Matt and I looked at her confused. We explained that we had been previously told the opposite. She was quick to correct this information.

Turns out he could stay with me; she just didn't have a bed or cot for him to sleep on. She said she could give us some blankets and shared that some dads curled up in the chair, on the floor, or in the bed with their significant other. It was completely up to us, but he was more than welcome to stay.

This was music to my ears and, I think, to Matt's as well. I honestly don't think he would have managed to get much sleep being away from me; he would have been worried and stressed the whole time. Plus, I wouldn't have been able to sleep either as I wouldn't have done well with him being away. I *needed* him there.

Turns out neither of us managed to get any sleep that night. Between the anxiety of not knowing what was going to happen, the possibility of going into labour at any moment, my constant back pain, the multiple trips to the bathroom, and sharing a tiny hospital bed . . . I am sure you can imagine.

THE ULTRASOUND

July 22, 2020 – Today was the day. Today we would get a clear picture of our little angel and hopefully figure out what was causing the polyhydramnios. We didn't have a set time, though the nurse said it would be sometime this morning. Someone from ultrasound would pop down and grab us when they had a moment.

At approximately 9 a.m., I had someone pop into the room and ask if I was LaCara. I confirmed, and she said she was there to take me to my ultrasound. Matt had only ever been to the eight-week ultrasound to confirm the pregnancy. Due to the pandemic, the hospital was not allowing additional individuals into ultrasound appointments. I asked if Matt could join, and she seemed surprised by my request.

"Of course he can," was her response.

She led us down the hallway, toward the elevator area, and continued past it. The room where I was receiving the ultrasound was maybe one hundred feet from my room. I am pretty sure it was the first room to the unit directly across from the antepartum unit where I was located.

We went into the room and the ultrasound technician introduced herself. I honestly cannot recall her name. By this time, I had met over a dozen individuals between the paramedics, flight crew, nursing staff, and physicians. I thought to myself, *Maybe I need to start making notes in my phone of everyone's names and roles.* (I did try this for a period of time, though it really did not help).

I got up on the bed and laid on my back. Within seconds, the pelvic pain kicked in, and I started squirming around. We anticipated this ultrasound would take approximately thirty minutes, which I knew was going to feel like forever due to the discomfort. Boy, was I in for a surprise . . .

This ultrasound was a bit different than the previous ones I had received. Their technology was much more advanced, and they had the ability to see everything in 3-D. Not only that, they were able to change the shadowing of the picture and even see what looked like the blood flow in some areas of our baby's body. How amazing!

Now, before I dive into things, allow me to just clarify something. Matt and I are not ultrasound technicians or trained to read these images. However, the 3-D option provides much more detail than a regular ultrasound, and I am quite confident that the majority of people would be able to interpret the images. Not only that, when you start seeing things that don't look good, your brain begins to go into overdrive and works to connect the dots. Having a background in healthcare isn't always a benefit in these types of situations. Instead of knowledge being power, in this case, I felt that it was crippling.

• • •

We started with getting a clear visual of our baby's face. Once the thumb was out of the mouth and hands out the way, we could see that there was something off. I asked the technician if what we were seeing was a cleft lip. She verified that yes, the baby had what appeared to be a bilateral cleft lip and cleft palate. I looked at Matt and smiled.

"That is totally fine, it is an easy fix," I said to Matt. He agreed.

I know tons of people that had been born with a cleft palate or lip, and a little surgery fixed that right up. This was manageable.

However, it didn't stop there. It was quite difficult to obtain a clear picture of the baby's chin. The ultrasound technician had to change the shading frequently as she scanned my belly to get different angles of the chin. It almost looked like there was a hole where the chin should be. We thought this was interesting, as both Matt and I had discussed how in the previous ultrasound, it looked like the baby had no lower jaw. Though, because we were not trained in reading ultrasounds, we trusted that if this were the case, it would have been noted by the trained professional(s) who read the scans and an appropriate follow-up would have been arranged. As shared previously, all prior ultrasound reports stated that growth and images obtained were normal without any abnormalities or anomalies found.

My mind began to wander and think about what this all meant. At this point, though, I was not yet thinking about the worst-case scenario, and my mind was working hard to try and put all the pieces of this puzzle together.

I began to feel completely overwhelmed and absolutely terrified about what we would be told about the images and our baby. As a side note, we still had no idea about the sex of the baby at this time. We requested that the team not reveal the sex of the baby to us, as we wanted it to be a surprise.

About thirty minutes into the ultrasound, an obstetrical specialist came in to speak with us and the technician. I was grateful, as this gave me an opportunity to move around a bit. Lying on that hard table on my back heightened the stabbing sensation in my lower back. After communicating quietly with the technician, the specialist relayed that there was a bilateral cleft lip and cleft palate. However, they noted other concerns and wanted to obtain additional imaging.

She shared that at this time, the most pressing concern noted was in regard to the lower jaw and that the scans showed that our baby wasn't developing at the rate they anticipated. The underdevelopment of the baby's jaw prevented the baby from swallowing amniotic fluid. Hence why I was experiencing extra amniotic fluid. However, there was more to it than that. The team was concerned that when our baby arrived in this world, he or she would not be able to breathe independently.

Immediately, my chest felt heavy and my stomach knotted up. Internally, I was experiencing complete turmoil. However, I am usually pretty good at playing it cool and not expressing my panic in such situations. After we received this information, I mentally checked out and could no longer hear what was being said. It couldn't have been much, as she left the room shortly after, and we continued with the ultrasound.

It took everything I had not to lose my shit. I couldn't even look at Matt. I do remember that at some point he reached over and grabbed my hand. Anytime I went to look at him, my eyes would fill up with tears. I did not want to cry in that room, so I avoided eye contact.

As we continued with the ultrasound, Matt and I quietly observed the scans. The technician started going over the other parts of our baby's growing body. She was collecting images and taking measurements of each limb.

Although the technician did not share her findings, we could see the measurements and notes made on the screen. Matt and I were quick to connect the dots that other parts of our baby may not be developing at the expected rate. Bone length varied from one side to the other, and the development ranged from anywhere between twenty weeks gestation to thirty-two weeks. The review and collection of these measurements lasted approximately thirty minutes.

Pictures were taken of our baby's tiny hands and feet. The specialist popped back in and pulled the technician out of the room. You know shit is serious when the team needs to discuss things away from you as the client. I should know. I am typically part of those discussions as a healthcare provider. To say that being on the other side of things sucked is an understatement.

We were told by the specialist that they noted some other concerns. Mainly the spacing in the baby's toes. There was a larger than expected gap between the first and second toes. Additionally, the angle and attachment of the thumbs did not align with what they would typically see in an ultrasound. This was not all though.

They spent that last part of the ultrasound focused on our baby's organs. The equipment they had allowed detailed visuals of the internal organs and even showed the circulation in different parts of the body. We watched as the screen lit up and noted what looked like blood flow flashing. Then I noticed that there were periods of time where it looked as though our baby's blood supply would be cut off to the lower parts of the body. This kept occurring as the technician took pictures.

Lastly, there was extensive imaging done on the kidneys. I cannot tell you what information was collected during the scan at this time; however, due to the baby not being able to swallow fluid, this meant that the baby's kidneys might have also been impacted by their other health challenges.

My back continued to ache, and I wiggled around on the table. As the ultrasound progressed, I did everything I could to try to keep my mind busy enough that I wouldn't stop to think about what was actually happening. My mind was operating on overdrive, though I have no clue what was actually going through my mind.

The specialist came back in and said that she was consulting with a team of different physicians and specialists. She relayed that a neonatologist would come to speak with us about our situation and that based on the scans, there was a long list of individuals who would need to be consulted and brought onto the team to review our case. Before leaving the room, she instructed the technician to get a couple more pictures of the baby's kidneys.

I wanted to get back to our room so I could curl up, cry, and just be with Matt. The scans didn't look good. The way the team responded wasn't good. This whole situation was what I would call a cluster fuck. When the technician was done, she wanted us to wait and see if the specialist had any further direction or information for us. After about fifteen minutes, the same individual who had walked us to the ultrasound room came in and escorted us back to the antepartum unit.

Walking back to the room exhausted me. I lost all my strength. My legs were weak; I just wanted to curl up on the floor and not move. Also, I don't know how it is possible, though I swear that during the time we were in the ultrasound, renovations were done to lengthen the hallway. Once we made it to the room, I felt a small sense of relief. Funny how that hospital room became something that was familiar. A safe haven almost. I needed something safe because deep down I knew exactly what was going to follow. Those fears I had stressed about in my younger years regarding all the complications that could occur in pregnancy were becoming my reality.

BETWEEN TWO EVILS

I've always been one to weigh the pros and cons of a situation before making a decision. Yet, for the situation we had been given, I struggled to find anything positive about it. Our baby was sick and would not survive this world without advanced life support and ongoing medical care. We could have the genetics team collaborate with us to explore what we were specifically dealing with, so that we had a definitive diagnosis. However, it didn't change the reality of the situation.

When Matt and I returned to the room, my eyes filled with tears and I crawled into bed. I can honestly say that I did not leave the room again that day. I just received the most heartbreaking news and I didn't want to see anyone, other than Matt.

I knew how Matt would feel about the situation. I knew his decision, without having to ask. Regardless, I asked. "What do you think we should do?"

He is a very logical thinker, like me. Here are the facts.

To explore an exit strategy, meaning we do absolutely everything possible to try to keep our baby alive, we would have to go through the following process. I would remain in the hospital until I delivered, as the team would work to prevent preterm delivery. The goal would be to get as close to thirty-six weeks gestation as possible, in hopes that the baby's body and organs could develop some more.

At thirty-six weeks, I would be placed under general anesthesia, and an obstetrical team would perform a Caesarean procedure on me. They would keep the baby connected to me via the umbilical cord, until they could secure an airway. This would require a tracheotomy. The hope being that this is a "short-term" solution (eight months to a year), depending on whether or not our baby's trachea developed enough to the point where they could breathe on their own. However, there was no guarantee that this would occur or keep our child alive.

Also, due to the lower jawbone not being developed, feeding would be an issue. A feeding tube would be required and feeding options explored. The baby would then require ongoing monitoring and medical support throughout this process, especially with the potential organ complications that might be present. This could require additional specialists and procedures. Our baby would need to live in the neonatal unit moving forward and would require multiple surgeries over a period of many years. Did I mention that there is no guarantee?

The lower jaw alone would require multiple surgeries. Because our baby did not have bone structure in both the jaw and cheekbones, as our child grew, more surgeries would be needed. Therefore, the first years of our child's life would include a series of painful procedures with lengthy recovery times and living in hospitals. The thought of having our baby go through this and setting them up for what could be a lifelong journey of surgeries and medical care was not what Matt and I envisioned for our baby. Both of us knew that neither of us would want to live that kind of life; why would we make that kind of decision for our child?

To boot, this wasn't even looking at the longer-term supports that would be needed. As our baby did not have external ear canals, surgical intervention would be needed. There was also the possibility that our child could be completely deaf. Speech and language therapy support would be required, in addition to ongoing psychological support to help our child and us through this journey.

As we live in a small, rural area, this would mean that we would need to relocate to a larger area to ensure access to the care, support, and treatments required to support our child through such an advanced journey. It would literally mean a change in everything we knew and again, no guarantees. No guarantee that our baby would recover, that our child would make it through everything, or that in the end our child would have a good quality of life. Pain would be inevitable, as our baby would require a long list of surgeries, medical procedures, and equipment to live. Even after all this, there would be extensive rehab and counselling to support our child in this world.

Alternatively, we had the option to proceed with a vaginal delivery and allow events to unravel without intervention. We would work with the team to ensure that our baby would not suffer during this process and be able to spend whatever time with our baby that we were gifted. I knew exactly what Matt was thinking, without him even having to say it. Because we are one and the same, and we have always been on the same page (book pun intended).

• • •

I honestly am not even sure how we made it through this next part. We had to share this information with our parents. Since the beginning, our parents had been purchasing items for the baby and making plans for when their grandbaby arrived. To be honest, I can't even remember these conversations or what was said, though Matt took the lead.

I will always be in awe over how he managed to compartmentalize the information we were given and proceed to get through every single day and be there for me. He remained calm and grounded through it all.

Together we managed to relay the information we received to our parents. I struggled with this because as soon as someone else started to cry, it would set me off. I didn't think I would actually be able to talk to anyone. Amazingly, there are times that I surprise myself. This was one of those times.

Our parents are amazing and were able to keep it together while on the phone with us. I do recall that the conversations were short and our parents were quick to end the call. I am pretty sure they, too, were doing their best to keep their shit together while talking to us.

Receiving this type of information is not easy to digest. On reflection, it would have been so much easier to have made a conference call with all our parents to share the news versus the five or six phone calls we made. Yet, at the same time, having to repeat the information made it real. The challenge was actually connecting with everyone, knowing we were all in different time zones, and we were reluctant to call our parents while they were working.

The first call made was to my mom at precisely 11:59 a.m. It lasted all of seven minutes and I knew that telling her would be the hardest. My mom is someone who is very emotionally driven and heightens my emotions and reactions. I must say, I was so impressed and proud of her. She showed incredible strength during our conversation and was able to keep it together. I am quite certain that immediately following our call, though, she picked up the phone and called my cousin Diana to let out everything she was holding back.

My cousin Diana and my mom have always been close. I am so incredibly grateful for the support that Diana provided to my mom during this experience. I am certain that the two of them could write a book just about the conversations they had during the time that Matt and I were in the hospital.

After talking with Mom, I figured telling the other parents would be a bit easier. Matt was surprised at how quickly I decided to call the parents and let them know. I figured there was no time like the present. Also, at that moment, I felt like I had it together. If I waited, I don't think I would have been able to form words and tell them what was happening. We continued to call all our parents. We had Matt's dad and stepmom, his mom, as well as my dad and stepmom to call. At the end of it all, I felt relieved. Yet, at the same time, I didn't.

Following the ultrasound, it was as though I stepped outside of myself for periods of time and was looking into someone else's life. Like, *Aw, this is such a horrible and heartbreaking situation. I totally feel for this couple.* Then it would hit me. *Oh, wait, this is my life. That woman is me. This is my reality.*

NO TIME LIKE THE PRESENT

At the end of 2019, I had a vision that I would create a coaching business and a social media group to support women in raising resilience to discover new ways of carrying hardship and adversity within their lives. The purpose of the Facebook group is to bring women together to support, inspire, and empower one another through expressions of sharing stories and experiences. This allows individuals to not only receive support, but also help other individuals who might be experiencing similar situations learn about other methods of carrying the weight of life's challenges, while also building a sense of community.

Of course, with me going through this journey, I decided it most appropriate to provide participants in the group with live updates along the way. Not everyone in my family understood my approach with this, though I saw it as a great opportunity to demonstrate what I envisioned for the group.

Since creating the group, I had found that individuals are often reluctant to share their stories and not keen to post in the group. To support and inspire engagement, I decided to start doing weekly interviews with women worldwide who felt comfortable sharing their stories and how their hardship or trauma has impacted their lives.

However, with being in the hospital and possibly going into labour at any moment, I figured it most appropriate to place interviews on hold. Besides, what better way to inspire others than to share the hardship that I was currently going through at the time, am I right?

I appreciate that this approach is not for everyone; however, I actually found it extremely therapeutic and felt so incredibly supported knowing that I had a group of women cheering us on and sending love and positive vibes. Having that sense of community can be key in situations like this. Also, this was a way for me to relay updates to others close to me. It took the pressure off of having individual conversations with people and allowed me to share my story as I was experiencing it.

In some ways, I think it made me more relatable. I have typically been the go-to person for support because I have demonstrated the ability to cope, manage, and conquer tough situations consistently throughout my life. Though the reality is it is a process, and I don't have my shit together all the time. However, I do work through it and work to cultivate a positive attitude when doing so. This was a great opportunity to share with others how I navigate through challenging situations and allow myself to be completely open and vulnerable.

This section provides an overview of what I shared online during my experience. I have not included all the information I relayed in my videos, so for individuals wanting the full run-down or to view these videos, you can find them in my Facebook group, Raising Resilience Movement, or visit my Facebook page, LaCara Biddles, to request access to this group. My first post was on Tuesday, after being admitted to Foothills Hospital.

July 21, 2020, at 5:20 p.m.

Hey Everyone,

I wanted to hop on here because I know this week and last week I have been a bit quieter than usual. I just want to bring everyone up to speed on what has been happening up until this point. The Friday before last, I went to the lake and started experiencing really bad pelvic pain. So, I've been trying to cope through that, going to the chiropractor, massage therapy, and had an appointment to go see an osteopath and my doctor.

Then last week I had a follow-up with my doctor and they decided they wanted to do an ultrasound because I am measuring huge. The ultrasound did reveal that I have too much amniotic fluid and so that resulted in a bunch of additional tests that needed to be done.

Today Matt and I were getting ready to head to Calgary and I was told that if anything were to change, to call my doctor. Of course, lo and behold, this morning I woke up and had some fluid leaking out of me. I called the doctor to let her know and about ten minutes away from the house, as we were headed to Calgary, I got a phone call from the doctor saying I needed to go to the Cranbrook hospital.

So, we took a bit of a detour and late this morning around 10 a.m. we got to the East Kootenay Regional hospital. They ended up taking some swabs and turns out I am leaking amniotic fluid. I am only thirty-one weeks pregnant so unfortunately the centre there is too small to manage if I deliver right away.

They arranged my transfer to a larger centre, and I am now at the Foothills Hospital. Me and baby are doing good. We are being closely monitored. I will be receiving an ultrasound tomorrow. They have told me that my membranes have ruptured, so it is a waiting game. Baby could come in the next twenty-four to forty-eight hours, or baby could be a week or two or three before arriving. Hopefully the baby does not come soon as I would like for the baby to get bigger and stronger, though they are giving me medication to support the development of the baby should I deliver early.

At the end of my video, I shared that I would continue providing updates moving forward. But I did not anticipate things to take such a drastic and negative turn. Regardless, I said that I would provide updates as we went along, and I wasn't about to back down from my word. So, my next update was the day after the ultrasound.

I could not bring myself to do the video update on the same day as the ultrasound and figured that I would know when the time was right. I couldn't sleep that night. I can remember watching the clock that was right above the bathroom door. Watching the clock became a pastime while we were in that room. It felt like we were frozen in time. I watched the clock with each passing minute. 1 a.m., 2 a.m., 3 a.m. During this time, I played out in my head what I was going to say during my next go live.

I figured if I went over it in my head, when I actually did the video, I wouldn't cry. I was wrong. When Matt ran down to the coffee shop Wednesday morning, I decided it best to just get it done and out of the way. I mean, who knew how long before or when I would be induced or go into labour. There is no time like the present . . .

July 23, 2020 at 9:37 a.m.

Good morning everyone,

I wanted to come on here quickly and give everybody an update on what is going on. As you can probably tell, my face is really puffy. The last twenty-four hours has been really tough, and I apologize because I don't know if I am going to be able to get through this. Ummmm . . . So yesterday I had my ultrasound and we were quite shocked by what was shared. Baby is not doing well and so today I will be induced. *Cue the crying*

I am sorry, I have played through this a million times in my head, hoping that I would be able to get through this without crying, but clearly that is not going to be the case. I have been on an emotional rollercoaster. As much as I would love to just show up and be able to walk through this and share this, this information is not easy.

Anyway, to give you the quick run-down, we've seen about six specialists. We have reviewed all the options that are available. Unfortunately, the baby is extremely ill and has not developed to where the baby needs to be; even if we were to make it to full-term, we would have a lot of complications. The baby would need a lot of support once delivered. The baby would not be able to breathe or anything on its own, so at this time we have opted to proceed with being induced and go down a palliative care approach.

Over the next twenty-four hours, I anticipate the baby will hopefully be delivered and we will go through that process. It has been extremely challenging, but I do need to say that I am at the Foothills Hospital right now and they have been absolutely phenomenal. I have never felt so supported in healthcare, and I work in healthcare. The team here has been amazing.

During the ultrasound, one of the specialists came in halfway through and told us what they were seeing so far. My ultrasound ended up being two hours long because they wanted to take a look at a bunch of things. And someone was constantly there throughout the whole thing to explain things to us. Especially since I was telling myself these little stories, even though I am not an ultrasound tech.

The team here has been amazing. It has been an interesting journey and it is one that is not finished, but at this point it is an opportunity to learn and grow.

I truly do believe that we are given certain experiences in our life and have a choice to make when presented with these. We can fall victim to the circumstance and create the mindset that life is happening to us, or we can take these experiences, give ourselves permission to carry them with us, and discover ways to move forward with them.

Having this type of mindset does not come easily, and it is a process. I had spent the past year prior to my pregnancy working to cultivate and improve my mindset. Life is so much easier and more beautiful if we can change the way we look at our experiences and life. Life is inevitably filled with heartache, misery, and so many horrible and ugly experiences. However, I get to choose whether I want to make these negative experiences the centre point of my life, or give myself permission to move forward with them and welcome joy into my life.

Losing our baby has been and will continue to be the hardest, most challenging and emotional experience that I live through. Regardless, I believe that Matt and I are the right couple to experience it. I believed from the beginning that it would not cripple our relationship in any way, shape, or form, and that it would somehow strengthen it. Because that is what we decided that we would allow. This was something we would work through together.

PRACTICE PATIENCE

I saw a picture and description of the word patience somewhere and felt it important to share with you the gist of what it said. *Patience is the ability to remain calm, no matter the end result. It is the ability of an individual to take action and turn any situation into growth. It is the ability of an individual to view things as an opportunity and trust that everything will work out in the end.*

Following the ultrasound, everything was a waiting game. Waiting for specialists to come speak with us; waiting for the next round of antibiotics to be administered; waiting for the nurse to come check in on us; waiting to see what was being served at meals. Watching the clock above the bathroom door became a pastime for both me and Matt.

Every time the nurse stopped in, she would relay that one specialist or the next would be coming up shortly. That Wednesday morning, we were expecting the genetics and pediatrics specialists, as well as a coordinator to come speak with us. We had not received a timeframe for the neonatologist or the NICU (Neonatal Intensive Care Unit) nurse. We would also be speaking with the obstetrical team again at some point in time.

In the meantime, I had more blood work drawn and my vital signs were closely monitored. My heart rate was dropping. Normal heart rate is between sixty to one hundred beats per minute. Prior to pregnancy, my resting heart rate was about fifty. Though, during pregnancy, my resting heart rate was closer to eighty or ninety, and since the ultrasound it began trending downward.

Just before 2 p.m., Matt told me that a family member had arrived at the hospital and was here to drop off a care package from her and her three sisters. Matt received a text saying she was here. Immediately following, the nurse popped in and said we had a visitor. The nurse asked if she would like for her to come into the room.

My immediate thought was that the hospital allowed me to have a maximum of two people visit me during my hospital stay. Should I need my mom in the near future, I didn't want them to decline my request. Due to our situation, the nurse didn't have any concern with allowing her to come into the room for a short visit.

At that time, we hadn't yet told the extended family what the outcome was for our child. I wasn't sure if she was aware of the situation. Matt had been texting with one of her sisters, as earlier that morning she had been asking what we needed as they planned on sending a care package. A few minutes before her sister's arrival, he provided her with an update on the situation.

When she entered the room, she was smiling and carrying a large reusable bag filled with goodies and a beautiful bouquet of flowers. I asked her if she had received a text from her sister. She said she had, but had not yet read the message as she had received it just when she was on her way up to the unit. She asked how we were doing, and I shared with her what was happening. She gave both of us a hug and together we cried.

Her visit was short. It was comforting seeing her beautiful familiar face. We were so incredibly grateful to her and her sisters for the care package. The drinks, snacks, books, flowers, lip balm, and lotion were perfect. My lips and skin felt so dry following our ultrasound, so they were put to use right away. That and the drinks and snacks.

I've always struggled with my body image and my weight. In my younger years, I went through some challenges with anorexia, bulimia, as well as binge eating. During a time when I felt like I didn't have control over anything, all I wanted to do was eat. It was the one thing in that hospital that I felt I had control over. Matt felt the same. The only thing keeping me from eating all the things was the fact that I didn't want to leave my room and the coffee shop offered only a limited variety of snacking items. However, both of us found comfort in the snacks that were included in the care package.

• • •

Around 3 p.m. was when things started to get busy. The neonatologist stopped in to speak with us. He shared that he had reviewed my pregnancy history, as well as the ultrasound scans. He discussed what things might look like, should we proceed with an exit strategy. He didn't sugar coat it and said that life would be extremely challenging for our child, as well as for us. Lastly, he relayed that there were no guarantees.

We asked questions about the type of care and treatments that would be required following delivery. We shared our thoughts and fears about the long, challenging, and painful road that our baby would have to endure if we selected the exit strategy. Then we shared that our hearts were leaning more toward a palliative care approach. He was very upfront with us and said that after reviewing the images and everything, he really felt that this would be the best decision and he was in complete support of a palliative approach. It was a relief to hear this, as anyone who has been in our position knows a part of you is always seeking confirmation that you are making or have made the right decision.

Following his visit, we had two obstetric specialists come and speak with us. They were aware of the situation and understood that there was a meeting scheduled for the next day. The specialists' panel was meeting first thing Thursday morning to review our case. If it was determined that a palliative approach was most appropriate, the obstetric team's plan was to have me moved to the labour and delivery ward then proceed with induction.

While the OB team was there, I quickly asked about my lab results. Earlier that day, one of the nurses said my blood work had returned and my white blood cell count was on the rise. Due to pregnancy, it is expected to be higher than normal. However, I was a little curious about what she meant when she said it was climbing. As my membranes were ruptured, I wanted to ensure this was reviewed and that everything was good.

Initially, when I brought this up, the OB was quite concerned and ready to take me upstairs immediately for induction. However, after he investigated some more, it was relayed that this increase was due to the medication I received on Tuesday. *Phew. An infection is not something I needed on top of everything else right now.*

Matt and I provided an update to our parents following the specialists' visits. The nurse told us that the genetics specialist would be arriving sometime between 5 p.m. and 7 p.m. However, they were not able to make it that evening, and we ended up meeting with them the following day.

In the meantime, we just sat in the room and talked. There were also many periods where we sat in silence, and that was okay too. It was a good opportunity to reflect on our situation. I've always been a believer that everything happens for a reason. Now, what that reason was I was not sure, though I needed to believe that I would walk away from this still in one piece; we both would. That was the only option available in my mind. I needed to show our baby that I was one strong mother . . .

That evening we ordered some food from a nearby restaurant and had it delivered to the front of the hospital. Due to COVID-19, individuals delivering food were not permitted access into the building, so Matt went down to grab the food.

When he went to come back in, he was asked for his ticket. Because he hadn't left the hospital at all, he didn't have an up-to-date ticket for access. Due to COVID-19, hospital visitors were given tickets stating they have been screened as clear and able to enter the building. He ended up going through the screening process again and was provided with a new ticket.

He returned to the room and we feasted. Tomorrow would be a new day and we would know more about what was to come and what the medical team thought about our case.

WISHING FOR A MIRACLE

S haring a hospital bed with someone else is not easy. Especially when my belly took up most of the bed. Somehow, both Matt and I were able to get a little bit of sleep that Wednesday night.

The emotional turmoil that I was going through allowed me to get a solid four hours of consecutive sleep. I was exhausted. I woke up around 3 a.m. to pee and started crying again. I have never felt so emotional and completely drained in my life. I was hoping and wishing the team would come back and say that things are not as bad as they initially thought. Oh, how I just wanted answers and to take control of the situation and ensure we had a positive outcome.

• • •

Early that Thursday morning, at about 6:30 a.m., Dr. B (the first obstetrician I'd met) came into the room. I hadn't seen her since the first day, when I was admitted to the hospital in the labour and delivery triage unit. She told me that she was headed to the panellist meeting, which started in ten minutes, and she wanted to check in on us. Neither Matt nor I can remember what specifically was said, though I can say I really appreciated seeing her. She had such a warm, compassionate, and calm demeanour. With her visit, I felt reassured that the team was working hard on reviewing our case to come up with the best plan of action to move forward.

• • •

You know, you hear of individuals who've been through these types of situations, though you never think that that will be you. I can remember having a conversation with a girlfriend a few weeks earlier, who recently delivered a beautiful baby boy. We were talking about one of her friends having received some blood work back, indicating that there might be the potential of her baby being born with cognitive deficits.

During that conversation, I encouraged her to help her friend remain positive and highlighted that regardless of the end result, her friend would manage and make the best decision for their family. Now that I was in this situation, all I could do during this time was hope for a miracle and ask myself over and over again, *Why is this happening to us?*

In January, we discovered that we were pregnant and didn't experience any negative outcomes early in the pregnancy. We had purchased and moved into our dream home in April. I was determined that the universe was in alignment and it was time for us to grow our little family. So why was this happening? Was the universe playing some trick? If so, I didn't like it.

We had put together a beautiful nursery. I had painted a mural on the nursery wall, mountains and wildlife to represent our lifestyle and home. Together Matt and I built a barn-style crib for the nursery. It went together perfectly with the mural and new flooring that he installed. We were so incredibly excited and eager to get the nursery complete prior to our little one's arrival.

The universe had different plans for us, though. Why? What was the lesson to be learned through this experience? Did we miss something? Was this karma? If so, for what? Why do shitty things happen to good people? Why do people who do not want children have them? Did this mean that we were not meant to have a family? *There must be a greater reason and purpose for this all. I mean, that is what society tells us, right? I want answers!*

My mind was in overdrive, yet numb and stagnant all at once. I asked myself all the questions. Then after cycling through all the questions, I would sit and think about absolutely nothing, feeling nothing, as I would step outside of myself. Then I would start with the questions again. My mind was on a circuit and I just wanted to get to the other side of this experience.

When Matt would ask what I was thinking, I would simply reply, "Not much." I didn't want to place all my thoughts onto him and bring him down into my little pit of mud. Truth be told, he knows me better than I know myself. He could read me. There were times when he would just reach over to hold my hand or get closer to me as my mind wandered. Even if he didn't consciously know what I was thinking, I am positive that his subconscious was reading my body, energy, and aura. Each of his gestures provided reassurance, comfort, and peace. His presence pushed my mind to refocus. I have him, my rock, my biggest supporter, my shoulder to cry on, my person. We may never get answers to the questions I was asking myself, though together we would help one another through this.

• • •

We received a visit from the on-call obstetric physician at approximately 8 a.m. We hadn't even had the opportunity to run down to the cafeteria to grab coffee yet. The panellists had met and a decision had been made. Everyone on the team was in agreement that a palliative approach in our case would be ideal. So much for that miracle . . .

The plan was that I would be induced later that day to proceed with a natural delivery and let nature run its course. Part of me felt relieved to have an answer, yet in the same breath, my heart was broken. Our baby would not be coming home with us.

Following the doctor's visit, a social worker popped her head in. I am not even sure we had time to process what was said. However, we continued to push forward and started the discussions about what needed to happen after the delivery and death of our child.

The local funeral homes in Calgary covered much of the costs in these types of situations. However, we did need to seek clarification on transportation, as our baby's remains would not immediately be available to us. The social worker assured us that she would speak with the funeral home about this in more detail and get back to us.

We talked about what support was available to us and how after we moved through this next part, she would visit us again with more resources and literature. I knew the process. There was a period in my nursing career when I had supported end-of-life care in the community. I knew exactly what the available supports back home were. The death of a baby is not common where we live, so there are minimal supports specific to these types of experiences. I would need to reach out to resources in larger communities.

I was concerned that we wouldn't qualify and meet the criteria to access support in Calgary, due to us being residents of British Columbia. However, the team did not feel that this would be a barrier for us. In hindsight, I should have asked for them to refer me to their pregnancy and infant loss program prior to my discharge. In that moment, though, I really wasn't thinking about the weeks that would follow. All I could think about was how I wanted to get through this and go home. I wanted nothing more than the familiar comforts of our home, our bed, and our dog. Unfortunately, that wouldn't occur for a few more days.

● ● ●

Matt managed to convince me that it would be a good idea to leave the room. Following the ultrasound, I hadn't actually left the room and had only travelled as far as the bathroom. I didn't really want to face the world. My motivation to do anything else other than cry was completely gone.

Together we made our way down to one of the cafés in the hospital to get some coffee. It had been a couple of days since I had been up and mobile, and I could feel it. I felt extremely short of breath and light-headed. We took it slow and I managed to get there and back to the room with only a couple of breaks needed.

Initially, when I walked out of the room, I felt overwhelmed and panic hit me. I didn't say anything to Matt about this, though; I simply pushed through it. I would have to leave the room and interact with the world again at some point, so might as well start today.

We passed other pregnant women with their significant others on the unit. I wish I could articulate how I felt in that moment. I wasn't angry or envious, though maybe a bit resentful. I hadn't yet delivered our baby, though I knew our outcome would not be a positive one like many of these other families. I was grateful that they would not have to endure what we would, yet also saddened by the fact that it was us who would soon live through the death of our child. *Why us?*

Although that first walk in the morning was a challenge, it felt good to get out of the room. After we had got back to the unit, I actually felt like I needed to get away from the area. So, we turned around and made our way back downstairs.

It was a relatively beautiful morning. The sun was shining, though we'd had some rain earlier in the day as the ground was wet and all the benches were soaked. Together we just walked around, soaked up the sun, and breathed in the fresh air.

When we returned to the room just before lunch, I had another set of vital signs taken. My heart rate remained lower than what it had been when I'd first arrived, sitting in the mid-fifties. However, I was not experiencing any symptoms due to this change. The nurse relayed that they were working on arranging my transfer to the labour and delivery unit; however, there was not a room or nurse available. They had called out workload in hopes of securing a nurse, though they were working short-staffed this day.

I totally understood and asked if they could just hook me up to the oxytocin in the meantime. I figured I wouldn't go into labour right away and even if I did, well, we could give Matt a catching mitt, and all would be well. In the smaller rural hospitals that I am used to, the nurses tend to work in all areas. I figured my request was feasible, though apparently that was not how it worked there. I would need to wait for a room and a nurse on the appropriate unit before they induced me. And so, we continued to wait.

We texted back and forth with our parents while we waited, each one asking if we needed or wanted them to come. My mom in British Columbia had a bag packed and was waiting for the word. Matt's parents in Ontario were prepared to fly out at a moment's notice. My dad and stepmom had previously planned to come to the area, so remained close by and available. However, both Matt and I felt that it would be more difficult to have them present during this time. If anything, I felt like it would have been most productive and supportive for them to all just meet and console each other throughout this experience.

Then, out of nowhere, I received a message on my phone:

Emergency Alert: *At 2:36 p.m. Mountain Daylight Time Thursday, Environment Canada has issued a tornado warning for this mobile coverage area. Take cover immediately if threatening weather approaches.*

Matt looked down at his phone to see he had received the same alert.

"Shit just doesn't stop" was the text I sent to my mom with a picture of the alert. Matt had also sent a picture to his parents.

Is this some kind of weird test from the man upstairs or what??? replied my mom.

Oh, for fucks sake... enough already!! Let's just throw in a tornado why not, was another message we received.

Matt and I simply laughed. I mean, what else are you going to do? No point in stressing over the weather at this point. We looked outside and what had been a beautiful sunny day just moments before turned into thunder and lightning with strong winds and hail. Fortunately, the location we were in does not tend to experience tornadoes, so we were quite positive that all would be well. My mom seemed to be of the same opinion and responded, *it's going to bypass you.*

By 4 p.m., the storm had passed. Matt and I were sitting in the room with an episode of *Modern Family* playing on the iPad. Then the genetics specialist popped in with her resident. They introduced themselves and we dived into a biology review.

Our meeting lasted approximately forty-five minutes, and to be completely honest, since our ultrasound appointment on Wednesday, my brain had not yet turned back on. The best way to describe me interacting with each of the specialists was like that saying "the lights are on though nobody is home." I was home, but just couldn't move forward from when we had received the news of our baby being ill. I managed to get bits and pieces from our conversations with the specialists, though Matt took on the role of being my eyes, ears, and brain.

The primary concern identified in the ultrasound was that our baby's lower jaw was not developed and was extremely small. This is a condition known as micrognathia. This characteristic alone can be the result of a long list of possible diagnoses, including Pierre Robin Syndrome, Trisomy 13, Trisomy 18, and Cri-du-chat Syndrome, as well as Treacher Collins Syndrome.

Essentially, the genetics specialist shared that she was seeing a lot on the scans and reviewed some of the typical diagnoses associated with the presentation and symptoms they saw in the ultrasound. We reviewed a long list of different possible diagnoses, though my brain can only recall a few.

We started with reviewing Trisomy 13 and 18, which are genetic disorders that result from having an additional chromosome (three versus the usual two). A child diagnosed with either one of these typically has a life expectancy of approximately one year. The ultrasound scans did reveal some consistencies that might be an indicator of either one of these, though there were other symptoms that did not align with this diagnosis, which are not typically seen with these conditions.

We discussed Treacher Collins Syndrome, which is a condition caused by genetic mutations for which there is no specific cure. Depending on the severity of the symptoms and characteristics that the child presents with, there may be different treatments available, such as craniofacial reconstruction, tracheostomy, bone conduction amplification (treatment for hearing loss), and the list goes on.

She shared that based on the scans and variety of symptoms our baby presented, the only way to obtain a concrete diagnosis would be through genetic testing. In our minds, we felt that by allowing the team to complete an autopsy, they would be able to collect more information to tell us specifically what and why this occurred. It would also reveal the severity of the symptoms our baby was experiencing, both externally and internally.

In addition to having the autopsy and placenta tested, we were both open to being tested and having our individual genetic make-up reviewed. Was our child experiencing this due to our genes? Did one of us carry a gene that we were passing on to our baby? Or maybe it was the combination of our genes together that caused this? The only way to know for sure was by moving forward with testing.

Over time, we will obtain more answers. However, genetic testing is a process, and it can take months . . . Looks like we have some more waiting ahead of us. In December 2020 we received an update from the genetics team that the genes evaluated so far have come back as unremarkable, meaning that genetically, there is nothing that would have caused our baby's symptoms. However, this test did not evaluate all genes and, therefore, further testing will be required.

Speaking with the genetics specialist was the last on our to-do list before proceeding with induction. Next came the part I was most anxious for. Part of me wanted to get it done and over with, knowing that our child would not survive. Another part of me dreaded it and wanted to delay it for as long as possible. So long as our child remained inside of me, our baby had life.

IT IS TIME

July 24, 2020 – I opened my eyes and looked at the clock. Another day had passed. It was 3 a.m. Friday morning. Maybe today would be the day I was induced. I slowly rocked my way out of bed, trying not to disturb Matt. We were both so tired and he looked so peaceful. I missed having uninterrupted nights of sleep. It had been many, many months since I had slept through the night without needing a pee break.

I came out of the bathroom and crawled back into bed, then the door to our room opened slightly. A nurse popped her head in and noticed I was awake.

"I am here to take you upstairs," she whispered.

It was time. I had tried to gather as much as I could and get organized the day prior, knowing we would be moving rooms in the near future. It was amazing how much stuff we actually had with us. We managed to load it all up and stack it in a wheelchair for easier transport. We followed the nurse to the elevator and up to our new room.

Matt unloaded our luggage into the corner of the room while I settled myself onto the bed. Time for a new set of vital signs. Immediately, she asked about my heart rate. By now I was even surprised as my heart-rate had dropped as low as thirty-eight beats per minute and had been maintaining in the low forties. You would think with all the stress my heart rate would be increasing, though it seemed to be dropping. She asked about my low heart rate, and I reassured her all was good. The nurses weren't too concerned so long as I remained comfortable and didn't have any symptoms due to this drop.

She took a look at my IV and said they would need to put in a new one. I kind of figured they would do this, as the size of the IV I had in my arm was smaller than what is typically inserted and used for pregnant women. My veins always look really nice to medical professionals, though they do not take being poked well and present as a challenge for many. For this reason, she said she would see if an anesthesiologist was available to insert one and discuss an epidural.

She told Matt he could wheel over the reclining chair that was in the corner and make himself comfortable. Matt was thrilled to have a space where he could recline and get comfortable. Side note: it wasn't until shortly before I was discharged from the hospital that I discovered that his chair was ten times more comfortable than the bed.

At about 4:30 a.m., the anesthetist came in to insert a new IV. Without skipping a beat, he managed to get it into one of my veins with ease. I admit, I was impressed as I've had other anesthetists struggle to get an IV in my veins. They are as stubborn as me.

Before he left, we went over the procedure for an epidural. Now, there are not many things I truly fear in life. However, a needle into my spine is a thought that terrifies me. And I mean *terrifies*.

I've had other individuals tell me their horror stories about epidurals and how it didn't work for them or how they ended up with a month-long headache due to spinal fluid leaking from the site after their delivery. I already fight with having migraines and tension headaches. I was not interested in having a post-epidural headache.

I actually discovered that this is not something that occurs frequently, though apparently only to everyone I know and talk to. He asked about where these individuals had received their epidurals. He suggested that maybe the individual who inserted those ones did not have the opportunity to do the procedure often. However, with over 500 babies being born every month in this unit, he reassured me that he did a lot of epidurals and had very few individuals in his career complain of this complication. One of the nurses even reassured me that she had never had a client experience this complication and she had been working there for nine or twelve years.

He also said that many individuals tend to wait until they are experiencing contractions before they agree to the epidural. Therefore, when they request an epidural, they are already in pain and have a difficult time sitting still through the procedure. This is what often results in post-epidural complications. Due to this, his recommendation was that we do it right then and all would be good.

He almost had me convinced, though not enough to move forward with it. I said I would wait and see how things went. However, in the back of my mind, I was having other thoughts. I actually felt that I deserved to experience the pain of delivering our baby because our baby was not going to survive. If there was any possibility that our baby would suffer, then I must suffer too.

At 5 a.m., they started the oxytocin. This medication is used to transition a pregnant person's body into labour. The way it works is that it essentially tricks a person's body into thinking it's going into labour, so it goes into labour. The nurses kept telling me early on that it can be really intense. I had no clue what this meant, so I just went with the flow. I mean, what else could I do at this point?

"Low and slow" is the motto I would use for this medication. The nurses started with a low dosage and slowly increased it over time. Approximately every thirty minutes, the nurse would come in, increase my dose slightly, and check the NST monitor. As the hours passed, the nurses would ask me if I was feeling any contractions; I wasn't. The monitor would have some readings, though I felt absolutely nothing.

My pelvis was still causing quite a bit of pain and I struggled to get comfortable. With the bed in this room, it was even more of a challenge to find a position that provided some relief. These beds have multiple cushions and pieces to them, which allows them to be pulled apart and rearranged during delivery. The leg part had the option to bend downward or be removed completely. The part that I sat on had its own set of cushions and was separate from the back and leg section. Then a small piece in the lower back area could be inflated and deflated for more support. I mean, I am sure it is great for when a pregnant individual is actually delivering a baby, though for resting and sleeping, definitely not. I wanted nothing more than to sleep at this point. I was emotionally and physically exhausted. Additionally, knowing that I would be pushing a baby out of me soon made me long for sleep that much more. I did not want to be awake for hours on end, pushing and pushing.

• • •

As time passed, the nurse continued to slowly increase the oxytocin. In all honesty, contractions were very faint and were not enough to grab my attention. Matt and I adored our nurse that day. She was such a kind and compassionate soul. She told us that she didn't think I would be delivering on her shift and that she was hoping to have the doctors come in and remove the last part of my plug.

Apparently, my membranes had ruptured, though there was still a partial block. This is why I didn't have the typical "my water broke" experience. She said that if the doctors came in and removed the remaining part, it would help move my body into labour and get the delivery process moving. She said she had asked the doctors a couple of times during the afternoon, though they were caught up in the operating room and would come check in on me when they had a chance. In the meantime, we waited.

We waited and the oxytocin continued to increase. Once we hit twenty units, a new order needed to be obtained to allow additional increases. I remained on twenty units for an hour or so before a new order was written. Once we had that, we were back to increasing every thirty minutes. I still wasn't feeling anything, though that would soon change.

THAT IS NOT POOP

My pelvic pain was becoming very aggravating. Finally, after hours of tossing, turning, and pacing, I asked Matt if he would give me a back massage. I mean, this is supposed to be one of the perks of this whole thing. Am I right? When pregnant, and especially during labour, all our requests should be granted. At least, that is my thought. Of course, he was more than happy to do what he could to help me out.

I lay down on the bed and turned onto my left side, with my head slightly elevated. Matt positioned a chair on the right-hand side of the bed and started massaging. It was more of a rub versus a massage, as the pressure caused more pain than relief. The rub felt incredible, though.

I could seriously get used to this.

Then, out of nowhere, a tsunami hit. I am not even kidding. I went into panic mode. I was convinced that I had just lost every ounce of amniotic fluid that was in me and it would harm our baby. *I mean, really LaCara, you know the ending to this story, so why am I thinking this?*

Matt's shoes were *soaked*. His pants were *soaked*. The bed was *soaked*. I even managed to soak through that thick blue pad on the bed and saturate the top blanket, top sheet, and fitted sheet. I had it all over the floor. I mean, *all* over the floor.

Fortunately for my nurse, who was on break, the covering nurse now needed to help clean this all up. The nurse told me not to move. I sat in my lake of amniotic fluid on the bed while she attempted to dry the floor so I could stand up and not slip. While she attempted to dry the floor, I sat there and continued to have fluid *pour* out of me. In my mind, I was thinking, *This can't be normal.*

After a solid attempt and about five minutes to try to dry the floor, she took a different approach and started laying soaker pads on the floor to create a path to the bathroom. As I made my way to the bathroom, I continued to leave a lovely trail of amniotic fluid behind me. Just as I got to the bathroom door, my nurse walked in. I am convinced I heard her laugh after she actually assessed the full scope of the situation and saw the amount of fluid I had released. She told the covering nurse that they needed to bring in the professionals for this mess. "Someone call housekeeping."

I had fluid everywhere. It was all over—on the bed, under the bed, to the bathroom, under Matt's recliner. Seriously, I don't think there was a dry spot in that room. I flooded my room. Apparently, this is normal when you have polyhydramnios to the extent that I did. I, however, was not expecting that. I mean, that was not what I was expecting when I experienced my water breaking. In the movies, it is more of a small puddle versus an entire flood and evacuation type of scenario.

Matt helped me to get cleaned up in the bathroom. I hopped in the shower. As I removed my saturated outfit, I continued to leak fluid. I do have to admit it felt so nice to get into the shower with the warm water. As I stood in the shower completely naked, I had nurses come in and out to check on me. It is true what they say: childbirth leaves you with zero shame or dignity. I am not even sure how many individuals had seen or examined my who-ha at that point.

Matt remained with me in the bathroom as I continued to have fluid pour out of me. He attempted to dry the floor in the bathroom while I stood there in the shower, waiting for the fluid to stop. I could hear the nurses talking in the room and warning the housekeeper, "Amniotic fluid is sticky, so try to avoid stepping in it." For the amount that was there, I am not sure that was even a possibility.

After about five minutes of just standing in the shower, I stopped leaking. So, I turned off the water and stepped out. Of course, just as I finished drying off, another gush of fluid came out of me and the floor was soaked again. So, back in the shower I went. This occurred three times before the nurse brought out the special pads.

I must say, this set-up made my ass look quite voluptuous. Like honey, I don't need to work out or get surgery, I just need to wear this and *boom,* we got booty! So, the key to this set-up is to first secure a pair of those really comfortable mesh panties you get from the hospital. Those of you who've gone through this, know exactly which ones I am talking about. Next, you want to take one of those blue soaker pads that are approximately seventeen inches by twenty-two inches and fold it into thirds. Now take not one but two maternity pads, overlap them slightly, and stick them to the blue pad. To secure in place, I recommend securing the pads first and then pulling the mesh panties over. Talk about feeling *sexy.*

Now, if you're like me, you may find that while reclined, you need a little extra absorption in the bottom area. So, what I did was take a second blue pad, fold it up, then positioned it so it overlaps with the first, and covered my ass. This way, if the first pad did not capture all my leakage, this second one would. Keep in mind, I don't think my leakage was the typical amount pregnant individuals experience. I had a lot of amniotic fluid. To put this into perspective, the normal amniotic index measurements for a pregnant person are up to twenty-five, and even after my membranes ruptured, I measured in at forty-eight.

Over the next hour or so, I had to change these pads every five to ten minutes as I was completely saturated. Over time, it slowed, and as it did, my contractions began. Once I had lost my fluid, I started to truly experience the contractions. Apparently, my body needed to create a tsunami before it could actually feel what was happening internally. After the fluid was gone, it was like, "Oh, that is what a contraction feels like. Okay, this is really not that bad. I don't see what the fuss is all about."

My contractions were nothing major at that point. It felt as though I had my monthly with some back pain and cramping. The cramping was consistent, though I found if I leaned forward in a chair, I didn't really feel anything. Besides, after the back pain I had experienced the past few weeks, this was a walk in the park in comparison.

The nurse kept coming in to check on me and asked if I wanted any medications for my pain. I didn't feel like I needed anything, though I did finally take some Tylenol around 8 p.m. as my neck muscles were in spasms at that point.

As the evening progressed, so did my contractions. Eventually, leaning forward in a chair did not help with the discomfort. I began to pace. As long as I was moving, I felt good. So I walked, back and forth, back and forth. Matt watched me, made a video or two, and took a couple pictures to send to our parents as updates.

As the time passed, my contractions became stronger. The nurse told us that the physicians would be coming in shortly to check and see how I was progressing, meaning they wanted to see how far dilated I was. This was at about 11 p.m. Almost immediately after, two physicians walked in. That night, there was a female physician with a male resident. They asked how I was doing and then got me in bed to check and see how far dilated I was. The male resident checked and reported that I was six centimetres. That was at 11:10 p.m. The doctors said that I was progressing nicely and would keep me running on thirty units of oxytocin for the time being.

Due to the dosage of the oxytocin and the amount of time that I had been on it, they said I was at an increased risk for hemorrhaging after delivery. Therefore, they would like someone from the lab to come up to draw a sample to complete a type and screen of my blood. I was agreeable.

The doctors and my nurse left. At this point, the contractions had me leaning over a chair, swaying my hips back and forth. A lab technician came into my room at about 11:20 p.m. to draw blood. At this point, sitting still was a challenge. Having a needle in my arm to take blood, while having what felt like back-to-back contractions, was definitely not comfortable. I did my best to keep my arm in place. She managed to draw three out of the four vials and placed a blood band on my wrist labelled with the time: 11:24 p.m.

Once she had left the room, I turned to Matt and said, "I think I need to shit," likely with a bit of concern on my face. The sensation came out of nowhere. So, I quickly disconnected myself from the NST and unplugged my IV monitor from the wall to hurry into the bathroom.

I sat down on the toilet, then I started thinking to myself. *What if this is not me having to poop? My mom had said that when she was in labour with me, she felt the sensation of needing to go to the bathroom; however, it wasn't poop that was coming—it was me.* I paused for a minute to really think about it before proceeding, and then I passed some gas. That was reassuring. I relaxed. *Oh no, the baby is not coming. I have to poop.* I proceeded and managed to do my business while contractions continued, and then something changed. I called out to Matt.

"MATT, CALL THE NURSE."

IT'S A GIRL

Matt called for the nurse down the hallway.
She came into the bathroom, and at this point, I was holding on to the grab bar, white-knuckled. I told her something wasn't right, and it *hurts*. She ran back into the hallway and called down to one of the nurses to page the doctors, stat. She came back into the bathroom and told me she was going to check to see if I was crowning. The doctors walked by the door as she was checking me, and she reported back to the doctors that I was not crowning.

She told me we needed to move me onto the bed, so I got off the toilet and a strong contraction immediately started. I stopped at the sink. With my right hand, I grabbed hold of the facet and turned on the cold water and told her, "It friggin' hurts." Meanwhile, my left hand/arm was in between my legs, with my legs crossed, trying to hold things in. I honestly do not remember what I was thinking at that point, though I had stuck my right arm under the cold water coming out of the sink and told the nurse I was going nowhere. The water felt good and I did not want to go to the bed. Nope, not happening.

It only took her a minute to convince me we needed to get to the bed. I slowly shuffled my way over to the bed, still with my left arm between my legs, while saying aloud, "No, no, no, no, no, no, no," as she guided me across the room. According to Matt, there were other noises

I was making; ones that he had never heard or thought I could make. However, there is no way for me to actually describe these to you.

On the way over to the bed, I noticed the doctors had set the room up with some equipment. They were gowned and ready for action. I, on the other hand, was not. I had made up my mind, this was not happening. N.O.P.E. The nurse helped me onto the bed with my legs spread. The resident checked me again.

"It is time to push."

I have no clue which doctor said this, though I did not believe them.

"No, I am only six centimetres dilated," was my rebuttal.

I was not ready to push. I was convinced that if I did, I would cause internal and external damage because I was not fully dilated. I don't know why I didn't believe them. They reassured me that it was time to push and that the baby was right there, ready to come out. I am sure I looked absolutely terrified at this point.

"I can't push. I am going to shit out my insides."

No joke, I literally said that. I was convinced that my insides were going to blow out of my bum if I pushed. That is the best way to describe labour. I have never had a woman describe the details of their childbirth to me, and I think it's probably for a good reason. Who the hell in their right mind puts themselves through this?! No. Instead, what they tell you is this, "Oh, it really isn't that bad."

What a bunch of liars. (Love you all.) Well, I am just going to be honest. It isn't fun. It sucks. And in that moment, when you're actually in labour, it fucking hurts and it fucking sucks. And yes, swearing is necessary. Plain and simple. I actually looked over at Matt and told him straight up, next time I am taking the meds. Kudos to me for even wanting to go through this all again. Just to give you a timeline for when this all happened, it was now approximately 11:40 p.m. Yes, this progressed *very* quickly.

The doctors and the nurse reassured me they would ensure everything remained in place and that nothing that was not supposed to come out of me did. I was satisfied with that and proceeded to push with my next contraction. I grabbed hold of Matt's shirt and wrapped it up in my left hand as he stood beside the bed, holding my leg. I took a deep breath in and started to push.

Between the pushing and my contractions, the doctors and nurse asked me questions.

"Would you like your legs up?"

"Would you like a cold cloth?"

"Would you like your baby on your chest?"

I couldn't think. I was so overwhelmed. Our baby was on the way, and we knew the outcome was death. *How am I supposed to think through all this?* This was supposed to be the happiest day of our lives, and I did not want to engage or be there at all. I wanted to hide under the bed, run away, be anywhere except in that room. I looked at Matt for answers. I am so grateful to Matt, as he was able to answer their questions. I just kept saying, "I don't know," as I had other things on my mind.

"What time is it?" I asked them.

"11:45 p.m.," the nurse responded.

Another contraction started, and I pushed. I was thinking about the advice my cousin's wife gave me. When in labour and you start pushing, remember to keep the pressure after you finish pushing so that the baby remains in place. I pushed and threw my head backwards against the pillow. The doctors directed me to push my chin to my chest and push hard. The contraction ended.

"What time is it?" I asked them.

"11:50 p.m.," the nurse responded, and another contraction started immediately again.

After asking for the time a third time, I finally told the doctors. "Today [July 24] is my sister's birthday and I don't want to have our baby today."

I didn't want my sister's birthday to end up being the same as our baby's, knowing the outcome was bad. There was always going to be milestones moving forward that would be a challenge, and birthdays would be one of those things. I didn't want her birthday to be a reminder of all the birthdays we would not be celebrating with our baby.

"Okay, LaCara, when you have your next contraction, do not push. Just hold on, relax, and breathe through it," the doctor directed me.

I nodded. I was happy to abide. Here's the thing, to say it and think it is one thing. To actually do it is a whole other story. I felt the contraction; the doctors and my nurse encouraged me to breathe through it. For the first portion of it, I managed to relax a bit and breathe.

"I need to push," I finally said, halfway through the contraction.

The doctor nodded to me and said that if I needed to push, to push. Go figure, that was it. That was my final contraction, and out came our baby. With it, a shit ton more fluid and immediate relief. The pain, the pressure, the burning sensation was completely gone.

"You are so strong," Matt said to me.

"What a beautiful baby girl," said the nurse, who was cleaning her up and getting her wrapped in a blanket.

"It's a girl," I said to Matt and smiled. I was so happy and yet heart-broken all at once. We had chosen her name the day prior. Kailani Mary Randall.

"What time is it?" I asked yet again.

Matt said, "12:01 a.m.," and Kailani's nurse said, "12:02 a.m." The recorded time of birth for our baby girl was 12:02 a.m. on July 25, 2020.

KAILANI MARY RANDALL

I lay in bed with my legs spread. I felt blood and fluid pouring out of me. The doctors delivered the placenta and did their thing to patch me up. Then they pushed hard on my uterus, and more fluid came gushing out of me. All I wanted was to hold our little girl.

While my nurse cleaned me up, Kailani's nurse brought her over wrapped in a pink blanket with a matching cap. When she came out of me, she didn't make a sound. That was the first mental note I made. *She isn't crying.*

When the nurse handed her to me, I immediately noticed her breathing. She had what is called agonal breathing. This type of breathing is not actual breathing, though—more of a reflex—and we see it frequently when people are in their last moments of life. Again, this is when knowledge can be crippling. I knew we wouldn't have much time with her. Her heart rate was only fifty beats per minute, which is very low for a newborn. She was tiny and absolutely beautiful. She weighed in at three pounds twelve ounces. Matt and I were in disbelief; this was our baby girl.

I started shaking. I was shaking so badly that I asked Matt to take her. I couldn't relax, and the hormones coursing through my body made it impossible to calm myself. The doctor ordered a dose of hydromorphone and the nurse administered it. I really didn't want any meds throughout this process, though I wanted to be able to enjoy the time we had with our baby girl. Soon after receiving the medication, I stopped shaking and was able to take Kailani again.

Together, Matt and I breathed her in and examined her tiny little fingers and toes. Everything was so tiny. How could one fall in love so quickly and love so intensely and immensely in a single second? I stroked her little cheeks with my finger and kept reassuring her that she would be okay, that she could let go, and that we love her.

I knew that we would manage and that she would always be watching over us. It was not what I wanted, though I had to trust that everything would be okay. I haven't a clue why, though I had to believe that we needed her looking over us moving forward. Even then, at that moment, I chose to believe that there was meaning to all of this and her death would not be in vain. What that meaning was, I had no clue.

Kailani's nurse came over and checked her heartbeat with a stethoscope again. It was now about 12:25 a.m. She looked at Matt and me with softness in her eyes and said, "I don't hear anything." That was it. Our baby girl had died.

As much as I dreaded the death of our baby girl, the one thing I wished for in the days leading up to that moment was that our baby would not suffer. I didn't want her to be in pain and I didn't want it to be a long and drawn-out process. My wish had been granted. I truly believe that this was why my heart rate had dropped so low in the days leading up to this moment. However, it didn't make it any easier. In less than thirty minutes, I had given birth, become a mother, fell deeper in love than I've ever experienced, and then had my child die in my arms. At times, life fucking sucks and is so incredibly cruel. This was one of those times.

• • •

The two nurses we had were absolutely phenomenal throughout this whole process. We had told the nurses prior to delivery that we would like pictures with our baby. Even after she had passed, the nurses helped us to capture our moments together. I just couldn't wrap my head around how these nurses were able to get through this with the other families also in our position.

One of the nurses shared that she and her family had a bunny that sat on the mantle of their home with the names of babies who did not survive this world. That is how she got through it. By remembering and honouring each of them. She shared that when she finished her shift and returned home, Kailani's name would be added. It broke my heart to hear this, though it also provided a sense of comfort.

At about 3 a.m., I could no longer keep my eyes open. The nurses brought in a bassinet for Kailani with a cooling blanket. I remember grabbing for the bassinet and pulling it closer to the bed so I could rest my hand against our baby girl. I couldn't stop the tears from streaming down my face. I have never felt so exhausted and defeated in my life. Before I knew it, I was out cold.

Matt told me he remained awake for about an hour or so after I fell asleep. He was so concerned and worried. He wanted to keep watch over me. He, too, was exhausted, and finally fell asleep in the recliner. Kailani remained in the bassinet between Matt in the recliner and me in the bed.

• • •

At 7 a.m., my eyes shot open. My neck muscles were tight and so sore. I turned over and looked toward Matt. There lay our baby girl's body between us. Reality sunk in all over again and I immediately started crying. I was ready to wake up from this nightmare. It had only been a handful of hours since everything had happened, yet it felt like it was a lifetime ago already.

Matt woke shortly following. Rather random, though: he found a scalpel in the chair with him when he woke up. We both thought this was odd, especially since the chair was nowhere near the doctor's sterile tables during delivery. We looked at each other and laughed. Thankfully, the cover had remained in place while he slept.

The rest of that morning is a bit of a blur for me. I remember feeling confused and heartbroken. There were also a *lot* of tears. I've never cried so much in my life. I was waiting and hoping to reach a point where there was nothing left in me. Anytime I looked at our daughter, it felt as though bits and pieces of me were being torn away. *How am I supposed to move forward from this? How am I supposed to survive this? Why is she gone, and I am still here? There is nothing right about this.*

• • •

Matt and I spent most of that morning alone, as the nurse had a very large amount of paperwork to complete due to our situation. As she worked her way through everything, she would pop in every once in a while, to check in or bring paperwork for us to sign. There was the documentation for her birth, her death, and the consent for autopsy that needed our signatures.

At some point, Matt went down to the coffee shop and so I took that opportunity to provide the Raising Resilience Movement community with an update. I couldn't bring myself to go live, so I did a recorded video and uploaded it right after. I couldn't even watch it before posting and cannot remember what exactly I said. To this day, I have not watched that recording and I have no intention of ever viewing it.

• • •

I felt so conflicted having Kailani in the room with us. Part of me wanted to wrap her up in my arms, though I knew if I did that, I wouldn't be able to let her go. When the nurse popped in later in the morning, I had to ask her to please do the footprints and then remove Kailani from the room. Having her there was too painful and heartbreaking. I mean, it was her body. Her soul had gone. Our baby girl wasn't in her body.

We kissed our daughter, breathed her in, and held her for the last time. Even though our daughter was not alive, and it was only her body that remained, the room felt so incredibly empty without her after the nurse took her. I had never experienced or felt pain like that. I had never cried so hard and loved so deeply in my life. Strangely, in that moment, I felt something else. A connection to Matt like never before.

In that moment, I felt as though our pain was one and the same. We held each other and cried. The room was empty. This whole experience put a hole in my heart like I've never experienced before. It is a hole that will never be filled. Yet, at the same time, my heart had never been so completely filled with a love so pure and radiant. I had never felt anything like it.

Although it felt like I wouldn't make it through this experience in that moment, a voice inside of me said, *Everything is going to be okay. This doesn't have to be tragic and horrible but can also be beautiful. I was exactly where I needed to be and everything in life would unfold as it should.* I wanted to trust and believe that voice, though in the face of such adversity, giving in to that belief and trusting things would work out was no easy endeavour.

• • •

As the day continued, everything started to irritate me. We had a visit from the social worker and called the funeral home to set up an appointment for the following day. I struggled to engage in that inter-action and to be honest, when she said she would see us the next day before our discharge, I immediately thought to myself, *I need to get out of here, today.* I did not want to see her again.

Then the woman in the room next to me went into active labour and I could hear her screaming. At first, I thought how amazing and grateful she must be to be meeting her baby soon. Then, I went dark. I started to resent her, whoever she was. She would get what I assumed to be a healthy baby while, meanwhile, we didn't. Our baby died. Why? How is that fair?

All I could think about was how all these people around me were having the happiest moments of their lives and here we were, heartbro-ken. *How is that fair? Am I a bad person? Is she better than me? Are they going to make better parents than we would?* Then I caught myself. *What kind of person am I to resent this woman?*

How could I be so angry and resentful toward the individuals around me when they have done absolutely nothing wrong? They deserve all the happiness in the world; we all do. Not only that, I didn't know her story. I didn't know the health of her baby. Besides, it's not like I would wish our experience on anyone. I recognize that I was envious of them and what I perceived to be their "healthy" babies. I needed to get out of this place, immediately.

The nurse came back into the room and relayed that we would be staying on the unit until all the paperwork was complete. She said that they were fully staffed and didn't have a lot of individuals admitted to the ward, so there was no rush to move me downstairs. Before she turned to leave, I asked her if they would consider discharging me today. She said she would check in with the doctors and get back to us.

At about 6:30 p.m., I received a visit from the original OB specialist that admitted me when I first arrived. She said that she supported me in our wish to be discharged, though she did not want us to head back to BC that day. We had an appointment with the funeral home the following morning, so travelling home was not an option. Medically, I was doing fine and the only thing that we really wanted to do at that point was rest. That was not something that Matt or I would be able to do so long as we remained in the hospital. At 7:15 p.m., the nurse popped in to take out my IV so we could leave.

As we were packing up and heading out, the two nurses who had supported us earlier that day during delivery popped their heads in. Strangely, it felt nice seeing them again. All the physicians and nurses I had seen during our stay told me they wished they could give me a hug. However, due to COVID-19 they kept their distance. Yet, one nurse, in particular, decided to make an exception and wrapped me in her arms before we left. I will forever appreciate and remember this moment. COVID-19 eliminated one of the most basic concepts we learn about in nursing school: human touch. I never truly realized just how important this was and what a difference it could make. It was in that moment I truly felt how our loss also impacted those in that room with us.

We said our goodbyes, left the ward, and headed downstairs. I stood outside the main entrance and observed all the people while Matt headed to the parkade to get the truck. There were staff, visitors, and patients heading in and out of the building. Some were sitting in the smoking area, while others walked around. I thought to myself, *How I wish I could go back to my "old" self. I wish that I could feel happy and joyous and energized. I just feel empty, heartbroken, and shell-like. I just want to wake up from this nightmare that I'm trapped in. Reality check, LaCara. This is your life.*

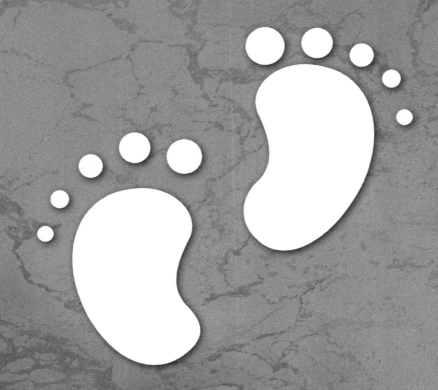

MY LITTLE ROO
By Lorraine Mahon

January 27 was the beautiful day we found out,
That a seed had been planted and turned to a sprout.
I was in disbelief as I walked through the airport,
As the text message came in and 'put me out of sort.'

Confused by the pic that came through from your dad,
Cuz he was always a joker, sending me funnies that he had.
This pic was a white stick, that had a 3 plus,
Not sure what I was looking at, or what was all the fuss.

I made a call to your mom as soon as I could,
She confirmed to me, this had to deal with her 'girlhood.'
I was so full of emotions and started to cry,
A big smile on my face, goose bumps up to the sky.

People around me, gave me strange looks,
As tears fell down my cheeks, I became unhooked.
I had longed for my daughter to have a baby one day soon,
The day was here, and I was an emotional baboon.

The ride home from Calgary was an extremely long one,
As I wanted to hug mommy and daddy, or just ANYONE!!!
You gave mommy a rough ride, of nausea and heartburn
A little bit of Nexium got rid of that concern.

As weeks went by, and you grew bigger inside mommy's womb,
You would kick her and stretch out and demand more room.
You had 3 ultrasounds, not one did you face front,
You must be a shy little one to pull off that stunt!

At 7 months you had your 3rd picture taken, with your head down south,
A side view of your face, with your little thumb in your mouth!
Mommy grew a big tummy and had pressure in her pelvis and ribs,
She painted you an amazing mural, and helped daddy build you a crib.

You have so much love coming from all directions of life,
Born into loving families, you will be guided through any strife.
With your mom's last ultrasound, at the 30-week mark,
A concern was voiced, and more tests were needed to embark.

You were being sent to Calgary, so they can get a better look see,
But mom started leaking that morning, and it wasn't pee.

She didn't make Cranbrook, when the call was made to the doc,
She said stop in the hospital there, you had lots of time on the clock.
They checked you out, and felt that a rush was needed to be had,
So, a plane ride to Calgary, in case anything went bad.

Daddy had to drive all the way in his truck,
A long lonely anxious ride for him, but he is a young buck.
Daddy met mommy at the hospital, she was in her room
They will be able to see all of you, and what's going on in that womb.

The 2-hour ultrasound was a disheartening result,
Further tests needed to be done, and a few people to consult.
Little Roo, you have so much love coming your way
But your stop here has had its hard challenges –like your airway.

Heaven is a better place for you to be, it has all the right things for you,
You can laugh and play, see relatives —there's a whole fun crew.

You will be dancing, and singing, and you can be twirled,
And you will be pain free, without a care in the world.
Forever you will be in our hearts, we will always love you,
Our little angel whose seed was planted, and where love grew.

I love you, *my sweet **'Lil Roo'**,*
Love your one and only, Gramma Lou

URNING A LIVING

July 26, 2020 – the day after the birth and death of our daughter Kailani.

Our meeting at the funeral home was scheduled for 11:30 a.m. I had been up since about 4 a.m., as my neck was hurting so bad that I had been in and out of the shower multiple times that morning to try to loosen my muscles. At 7 a.m., I hopped in the shower yet again, as my neck and back muscles were in spasms. Between my neck and constantly needing to change my pad every hour from the bleeding, there was zero sleep to be had. By about nine that morning, Matt finally woke. He is usually an early bird, though with everything going on, his body clearly needed some rest.

I can remember lying on the bed, watching him get ready. All I could feel was the burning sensation in my back and neck at this point. Emotionally, I felt completely numb in that moment, though I knew that would surely change.

After we got ready and all packed up, we headed down to the main lobby to head out to the parking lot. There was someone sitting on the couch in the main lobby area. Prior to this experience, I didn't really pay attention to people in my surroundings when out and about, though now I seemed to be absorbing everything. *Who is smiling, laughing, and enjoying life? Who looks bored, uninterested, or disengaged? Who looks heartbroken, defeated, and disoriented?* I was definitely the latter.

We headed out to the parking lot and packed up the truck. As I went to get into the passenger side, I managed to open the door and the corner went right into my thigh; it hurt, though not as much as my neck. I didn't realize the damage done to my leg until a day or two following. That is the visible scar that I will carry with me as a reminder of everything that I experienced that day.

We immediately started heading to the part of the city where the funeral home was located. On the drive there, I began to cry. Matt asked me if I was okay.

"We didn't pack anything meaningful that we can have cremated with Kailani. All I have are new items of clothing and some stuff from mom because my clothes don't fit. Do you have anything?"

"A hat?" Matt replied.

We never prepared for this type of outcome.

"Maybe there will be a store by the funeral home we can stop at and they might have something?" Matt suggested.

That sounded like a good idea. Maybe we could find duplicates of things we had at home for our baby girl. We were grateful to find a complex with a couple of stores only a couple blocks away from the funeral home. Of course, the store didn't open until 11 a.m., so in the meantime, we managed to find ourselves some breakfast and a coffee while we waited.

As we sat in the vehicle, waiting for the store to open, I observed the people around us. Laughing, joking, playing around. I wanted them all to suffer. This thought made me feel even more guilty and angry. Why on Earth would I want others to feel this way? I envied them. *I want everything to go back to how it was supposed to be. Back to us expecting a beautiful, healthy baby and building an amazing life with our child. Instead, we get to feel empty, heartbroken, and miserable while the world around us continues on. How can we just continue on? How can I go back to my life? How can I go back to living a happy life? How does someone live with this?*

The clock on the radio inside the truck changed to 11 a.m. It was time. We went into the store and immediately headed for the children's section. Matt had asked me before we went into the store if I wanted to stay in the truck. I refused, partly because I felt like we needed to do this together because we are a team. Though also because I didn't want to be alone in the truck. I just needed him near me.

We managed to find three items of meaning: a onesie, a stuffed animal, and a book. The onesie we found was identical to the very first one ever purchased for our baby. It was given to us by my mother. There was a picture of a baby bottle with "I'll have a bottle of the house white," on the front. This would do nicely.

The second item we found was a stuffed elephant. I have always related to this animal and it holds a lot of significance to me. I have elephant décor throughout our home, plus one tattooed on my back, and, of course, a stuffed one in the bedroom. We were not able to find the same one that I have, though we did find one that I was satisfied with. I ended up purchasing the same one a couple of weeks later, as I felt I needed it to feel closer and more connected to Kailani.

The third item, *Love You Forever* by Robert Munsch, was selected by Matt. Matt didn't know this at the time he selected the book, but Robert Munsch wrote it following the experience of two stillbirths. Coincidence? I think not. Matt selected this book as he felt it represented the unconditional love between a parent and child.

After we had the three items in hand, I had myself a little meltdown. Yup, right there in the middle of the store. Usually, I would never allow myself to express emotion like that, especially in a public place, but this is something I have come to accept as part of a new reality over the months following. The more I try to avoid or hide my grief, the worse things get. So, word from the wise: just let it happen and know that it is okay to feel these things.

After I had my little cry into Matt's chest, we headed for the checkout and back to the truck. We drove the two blocks over to the funeral home and put the truck in park. We were one of the only vehicles in the parking lot.

My eyes and cheeks overflowed with tears as I squeezed Smudge (the stuffed elephant). I didn't know if I could actually go in there. It made everything so real. I was still just hoping it was all a dream and I would wake up. Matt told me he could do this part on his own if I couldn't go in. There was no way I would ever make him go through this alone.

Together, we walked through the doors.

We were taken to a conference-type room and sat down at a large oval table. I sat at the far end of the table, farthest from the lady we were talking to. Matt held my hand. At the front of the room she had a large television and asked if she could share her computer screen with us for ease. We agreed. Then we started going through all the documentation. My name, his name, our address, our daughter's name, birth, weight, time of death, etc.

Being there and having the conversation made it all so real. This wasn't a nightmare that we would wake up from. We actually had to discuss the arrangements and processes we wanted for our daughter's body. How f'ed up is that? Parents should not be doing this for their children. *Ever.*

On a side note, I cannot imagine working in a funeral home. I imagine it might be quite depressing. I suppose there is only one positive thing about it; if you're looking for job security, it is lifetime guaranteed. Pun intended. Moving on . . . I could go on with these puns . . . though, in all seriousness, this was a hard friggin' day.

I have to be completely honest here. For those that know me, and I mean really know me, they know that when I am scared or nervous, I use humour as a way to interrupt situations that I am uncomfortable with as a means to cope, detach, and avoid them. Yes, I very much resort to flight mode. With that said, prior to Kailani's birth, Matt and I were having a conversation about how we would be selecting an urn for our daughter after delivery. At that time, I joked about using a coffee tin (as in the movie *Due Date*). I know some people are thinking, "Like, really LaCara!?!" Like I said, humour is one of my coping mechanisms.

Yet, I remember standing in front of a wall with a bunch of urns and thinking, *None of these are good enough. There are so many options. Various shapes, sizes, and materials; wood, marble, metal, large, small, adult, infant, etc.* I felt totally overwhelmed and didn't feel like any of them met my expectations for our daughter—nothing would. I mean, really, all I wanted was for her to live. Plain and simple. *If I select an urn, it just makes it that much more real.*

I looked to Matt for direction. *I mean, our daughter is not coming back to life and we have to select something.* We managed to agree on an infant-sized urn made out of bronze, square, and plated in pink. As we were able to select an engraving, we looked over the options in the magazine provided to us (yes, they have a catalogue for the dead). We selected the font type and picture that would go on her urn.

Immediately, Matt and I selected a picture of a teddy bear holding a daisy and the most elegant font that was available, which would read:

Kailani Mary Randall
July 25, 2020

We were almost done.

Now for the costs. Due to our situation resulting in the death of our baby, the funeral home covered the cost for the majority of things and discounted others. There were only three things that were included in the final costs: the urn (which we received a discount for), the provincial fee you pay when someone dies (yes, we have to pay to die), and the transportation costs to get our daughter's ashes home.

"Will that be cash, credit, or cheque?"

That was that. We loaded back into the truck and I cried some more. Time to head home.

AN ANGEL'S GIFT

Matt decided to drive through the park on the way home. For those not familiar with the area, there are two options for us to get home. The first, straight roads and nothing but fields to look at and the second, the park. The park is absolutely stunning. For anyone who has not driven Highway 1 through Banff, then down Highway 93 to Radium, you need to do this. The views are spectacular, and the water is so clear and blue. It had been a couple of years since I had travelled this way and I was looking forward to the scenery. Unfortunately, I didn't get to enjoy much of it.

We stopped a few miles outside of Calgary to fuel up. Once we got on the road again, Matt gave his mom a call. As we started to get closer to the mountains, service began cutting in and out; the connection was lost. We sat in silence with the radio playing. There was only one thing on my mind. I kept repeating her name over and over and over in my head. I longed to have our daughter back and wished she was with us. *Kailani, Kailani, Kailani, Kailani, Kailani*—I am not sure why, though I thought maybe if I said her name enough times, I might get a sign from her.

Then, before we even got into the mountains, I passed out. The emotional and physical pain finally caught up to me, and I couldn't keep my eyes open any longer. I needed to sleep.

Suddenly, I was awake. I immediately looked at the time. It read 4:44 p.m. I thought to myself, *That's a new one. I haven't seen that sequence of numbers before; I wonder what they mean.*

Now, before I go forward and tell you what 444 means, I want to provide a bit of a background on numerology and angel numbers. Prior to my pregnancy, I had not noticed number patterns or felt a strong spiritual connection in life. However, in the year prior to my pregnancy, I started to focus more on building my spirituality and learning about numerology. Then, following the death of our daughter, my spiritual connection continued to expand at a rapid rate. I have come to feel and discover as though this whole experience was meant for me in this life. The signs leading up to her death and following are just too significant for me to ignore. So allow me to explain a bit.

This is a very basic and simplified overview of numerology and angel numbers. If you're interested in learning more, I would definitely recommend doing some research or following up with someone who specializes in these areas.

Numerology

The study of numbers in a person's life has been around for many years and its origins remain a mystery. The way it works is that our lives have numerical patterns that are affected by our date of birth, our names, and other factors. If the numerology of one's life is broken down, it can help one better understand one's purpose and who one is as an individual in this world.

It wasn't until about six months prior to my pregnancy that I was introduced to this concept and began to look into it some more. I actually had plans to have a full numerology report completed back in September 2019, as this concept absolutely fascinates me; however, I never moved forward with this as I had other priorities at that time.

Angel Numbers

Angel numbers are a specific sequential pattern of numbers and these appear to individuals repeatedly. In numerology, each number holds a vibrational energy or frequency that represents a specific meaning. Angel numbers focus more on how frequently these patterns of numbers show up and serve as a means of communication or a sign. What kind of sign, you ask? I will demonstrate by sharing what has been occurring for me.

• • •

Now, angel numbers for me present as 111, 222, 333, etc. These began to show up multiple times throughout my day. I was aware of them prior to my pregnancy, though I didn't really notice them until I became pregnant.

Now, here's the thing. When I discovered that we were pregnant, I started to question whether or not I was on the right path. *Is this what my life mission and purpose entails?* This was a big question for me, as I was never one who was one hundred percent, without a doubt, committed to the idea of having children. I mean, with all the negativity and horrible things that happen in our world, why would I want to bring a child into it? This clearly was my negative inner thoughts taking over.

Matt told me from day one that he didn't envision himself being a father and had maintained that position until our pregnancy. I can remember walking through Walmart with him one day, past the baby clothing, and told him that I did plan on having two children one day. So, if he wasn't on board with that, he should hit the road. Even though I said this then, as time passed, I was not sure if parenthood was really what I wanted; I was okay with things either way. However, Matt and I both value our independence and our live-for-the-moment lifestyle, something that would become a little more of a challenge if we introduced a little one to the mix. Therefore, a lot of questions started to pop into my head and I started questioning what my new path or life journey would entail.

As I began questioning things, the sequence of numbers I most often noticed was III. Now, this sequence of numbers, from my understanding, is most closely related to manifestation and the law of attraction. As part of my pregnancy journey, there were specific goals I felt I would be inclined to achieve during my time away from work. So, I set specific goals and dreams for this period, with the intention of achieving each of them.

This sequence of numbers is a sign that one's intentions are manifesting into reality. This means that intentions must be carefully considered, to ensure that one is not attracting negative outcomes or undesired outcomes in one's life. I admit, I was able to create a very clear vision of what I would be creating after I delivered our baby. However, there were times when I doubted myself and my abilities to enter parenthood.

For a very *short* period of time, I actually believed that I brought the outcome of our daughter's death on myself. Allow me to explain. I can remember, around the five-month mark (when I started developing more fluid), wondering if this was truly the life I wanted. *Did I really want to experience motherhood? Would I make a good mom? Was I ready to give up our current lifestyle of travel, concerts, and spontaneity? Would I be able to be the role model that our child needed to grow into the best version of themselves?* I had a long list of doubts, as I am sure many parents experience before their child arrives in this world.

I honestly wasn't sure. The thought of parenthood terrified me, and for a moment, I thought that maybe it wouldn't work out and something would happen. And that thought absolutely terrified me. That thought solidified and grew the connection I felt to our baby and the desire I had to be a mother. That was when I began to see a new sequence of numbers: 222 started appearing everywhere during the period when I was doubting myself. It provided me the reassurance I needed, as this sequence indicates you are exactly where you need to be and to trust that everything is working out the way it is intended.

With that said, it made me stop and think that maybe my thoughts were what manifested what was now our reality. And although I do not believe that I created or manifested this outcome, I have developed the belief that this journey and experience was meant for us.

So, 444, what does that mean? I immediately grabbed my phone and opened my photo app. I had previously taken a screenshot of an angel numbers cheat sheet from an individual I follow on Instagram: 444 – "you are completely surrounded by angels." This message is intended to help those that are struggling through a difficult situation. It provides reassurance that if a difficult decision has been made, to remain confident and leverage your inner strength to move forward. Believe in yourself and your capabilities; chase your goals and dreams until you reach them. Most importantly, everything is going to be okay.

I am convinced it was my little angel communicating with me. This tragic thing that happened in our lives absolutely sucked, though it didn't have to be "tragic." It could be beautiful. There are always lessons to be learned in life and everything has beauty, even if we don't see it at first. I was determined to turn this experience into wisdom and allow it to build me up instead of tear me down. In the following weeks, more gifts appeared, and it began to feel like everything in my life was working out the way it was supposed to.

Sweet Mama

A couple days after I returned home, my best friend Tsarina, with whom I grew up, sent me a message saying she had written something for me that morning (July 30, 2020). Now, Tsarina has always been incredible with words and formulates beautiful poems about the complexities of life. She shared that the year prior she had hoped to write more, though she had been experiencing a block until that morning. She was sitting outside, listening to the birds and looking at her flowers, thinking about me and Kailani. Out of nowhere, the words just started flowing and the poem "Sweet Mama" was created.

Now, when I first received this gift, I didn't give the title much thought. However, after about a week or two had passed, I realized something interesting. When I was in the hospital, I received a message from a co-worker and friend, encouraging me to reach out to someone who had also experienced a neonatal loss some years ago and who worked at Foothills Hospital. While in the hospital, I exchanged text messages back and forth with this individual and she became a key support during this time.

In our messages, one of her requests was that I share the name of our daughter or son, as she would be honoured to celebrate the birth of our little one. Immediately following the birth of Kailani, this individual began to refer to me as "sweet mama" in all of our communications.

When I talked to Tsarina about how she came about selecting the title and using "sweet mama" in her poem, she said it was something that came to her without any rhyme or reason. Funny how two individuals that I kept in close communication with during this time, though they had never spoken to one another and were not aware of the other, came to use this term. Coincidence? Not in my opinion; it was another sign.

Willow Tree

During my pregnancy, my two nieces, aged eight and nine, were over the moon about having a baby on the way. Of course, with both of them being female, they were hoping for a little girl, so they could do all the little girl things and babysit her. So, when things took a turn, I asked my mom to speak with my brother to determine how they would share this news with them.

They were crushed. Interestingly, my oldest niece told her mom that she wanted to get a gift for us. It wasn't until about four weeks after Kailani's birth that I got to see her. When she came for a visit, though, she presented me with the most beautiful gift. It was a sculpture of a mom, dad, and baby; "Our gift" is the name of this piece and it represents new beginnings.

Susan Lordi is the artist who hand carves the original figurative sculptures of Willow Tree. The meaning of these sculptures is meant left open for interpretation by the giver and receiver of these beautiful pieces. However, the sculptures represent and express emotions such as love, healing, closeness, hope, and courage.

Where is the message in this gift, you ask? Following Kailani's birth, I was introduced to an online group for pregnancy and infant loss called Tiny Footprints. This group is a place for individuals to share stories, find support, and talk about different resources and information. The first post I came across was a video about another individual's story of neonatal loss. Within that video was this same sculpture, placed in a bed of flowers. Coincidence? I think not; it was another sign.

I could go on and on about these signs: finding myself in a field of butterflies; rainbows appearing randomly in pictures or in my environment during low times. Having a dragonfly land on my head and sit with me awhile, only to have a baby dragonfly land on my stomach shortly following. So many different things that have never happened to me before. Although this heartbreaking thing happened, I consistently received reassurance that everything was going to be okay, and everything would work out exactly as it needed to. That is not to say that the weeks and months that followed were not difficult to get through. The weeks and months following the death of our baby girl were the most challenging days of my life in so many different ways. I thought getting home would make things better for me, though as the saying goes, "things must get worse before they get better."

SWEET MAMA
By Tsarina Posnikoff

I've cried too many tears today,
They fall down in your name.
My heart feels so empty now,
The tears extinguished my flame.

I did everything I possibly could,
To ensure your body grew.
We ended up with a few short minutes,
With a love that was so new.

You passed away peacefully,
I held you over my heart.
A thousand tears fell down my cheek,
I never want to part.

The day I said goodbye to you,
It was the hardest day I ever knew.
It will take time to understand,
It will take time for us to pull through.

I'm with you now sweet mama,
I'll be the wind upon your cheek.
I will hold your heart sweet mama,
I'll give you strength when you are weak.

There is no pain sweet mama,
Just love, light and laughter.
There is only beauty sweet mama,
Butterflies to chase after.

Please don't cry anymore sweet mama,
I'll be waiting here for you.
When that day comes sweet mama,
I'll walk to the gates with you.

An angel we will forever know,
Her memory is on our mantel,
She will always be remembered,
Her name is Kailani Mary Randall.

THERE IS NO PLACE
LIKE HOME

After waking from my nap, I found myself in quite a bit of discomfort. My neck and shoulders were so tense; I couldn't find a comfortable position in the truck. I managed to push through, without making any additional stops. I just wanted to get home, as did Matt.

We turned left off the highway onto the side street toward our house. Home was only thirty seconds away. Matt put the truck in park and immediately went to open the door. Gibson was inside, as my mom had dropped him off just twenty minutes before. I waited in the truck, as we weren't sure how Gibson would respond with the excitement of our return. After a moment, I managed to manoeuvre myself out of the truck and then froze.

Due to sitting in the truck for so long, blood started flowing out of me once I stood up. I needed a bathroom immediately. I started walking toward the front door and Gibson approached me. His tail remained down, wagging between his back legs. He gave me a couple sniffs and I managed to get a few pets in before he ran back over to Matt. He seemed a little unsure of me and kept his distance. I am sure he could sense something was wrong.

The house felt empty and cold. My mom had gone through and moved all the baby stuff into the nursery. On my way to the washroom,

I noticed she had used a sheet to cover the crib that Matt and I built for Kailani. I wanted to cry so badly, though all I could feel was the physical pain in my neck and back. I just wanted some relief; when will this pain end?

I jumped in the shower. I needed to clean up and I was hopeful the heat would help settle my tense muscles. Once I finished, I crawled right into bed. Honestly, all I wanted to do was remain in bed and cry. Actually, that had been my plan all along. Simply stay in bed, do sweet fuck all, and just allow my emotions to pour out of me—something I would never have done in the past. Go figure. My body had other plans for me.

The pain was escalating. I could not find a comfortable position. Staying in bed was not an option. Although walking helped distract my mind a bit, it didn't lessen the pain. However, walking was really the only thing I could manage to do at that point.

As the days and nights passed, all I could think about was our daughter. *Kailani, Kailani, Kailani . . .* I just kept repeating her name in my mind while I paced in the kitchen and living room. I felt so incredibly tired and weak. My mind needed a break, though it kept replaying our reality over and over. I wanted to cry; I needed to cry. Yet my muscles were becoming more tense and my pain was climbing. During the day, I tried showers, baths, massages, stretches, acupressure, and meditation. The pain worsened. Nothing was helping to alleviate it. *How is this even possible?*

I mean, I tried using natural remedies and staying away from medication. Though as the days progressed, I started trying Tylenol, Aleve, Robax, T3s, etc. I was trying all the over-the-counter medications and various combinations to try and find relief. I was well over the daily dose for a few medications to try to find resolve. None of these were helping. After four days of not sleeping and constant pain, Matt finally persuaded me to go see a doctor.

I was able to get an appointment for Thursday morning with one of the maternity physicians. I was really hoping that I wouldn't have to go to the clinic, recognizing that I would have to face my co-workers (something I was not yet ready to do). I wanted to remain in hiding.

Matt came with me and I made a point of wearing dark clothing, keeping my hair down, and wearing a baseball cap to try and keep covered. We waited in the truck until the very last minute, as I knew there would be an increased chance of me running into individuals if I was in the waiting room. At this moment, I was quite happy that Matt had not met many of my peers; they wouldn't recognize him.

We walked onto the unit and I smiled at the receptionist, who happened to also be a good friend of mine. I sat down, and she ran over and gave me a hug. Immediately, I started crying. Fortunately, the doctor came to my rescue and called me into his office. He apologized for our loss and asked how I was feeling. To be honest, I didn't even feel like I had just given birth to a baby. My lady bits felt fine; all I could feel was my neck and back.

I explained to him the muscle pain I was experiencing. We discussed what options were available to me, including injecting a relaxant directly into my muscles—this procedure might require multiple treatments. Alternatively, we could try to force me to sleep using diazepam in an attempt to allow my muscles to heal. I opted to try the sleep approach.

I had taken this type of medication in the past for muscle spasms and found it to be very effective as I was able to relax. This time around, due to me not getting any sleep and the amount of pain I was in, it was agreed that I would take a bit of a higher dose. I actually ended up having to double the dose prescribed, as it did not provide any relief and I was not able to relax or sleep. After doubling the dose, I finally managed to sleep for three consecutive hours; this was more sleep than I had got in the past four days combined. Sometimes, you have to take the small wins where you can. This was one of them.

This relief allowed me the opportunity to transition my focus away from the physical pain I was experiencing and begin the reflection process of this experience. I started to explore grief a little bit more and ways to find meaning in everything I was experiencing. As a reader, I decided to go online and see about what other resources were available about neonatal loss. I was surprised to find that there are a limited number of resources. I mean, I now completely understand the challenges of writing about such experiences. I have pretty much bawled through writing every part of this book.

There are books written by physicians and specialists in the area of neonatal loss. Reading a textbook or going through the five stages of grief felt so cold and was not what I needed at that time. Besides, with my nursing background, I went through many of these concepts in school. I was looking for something different.

I wanted to know how other people managed through such a horrible loss and were able to come out of it on the other side, living a happy and fulfilled life. What were their stories and their suggestions? I needed to know the key to grief and life without my baby. I felt so frustrated and disappointed that I couldn't find what I was looking for. At that point in time, I stopped my search for such a resource and allowed myself to dive into my grief. I continued with my reflections and searched for meaning in the ways I had done previously, using resources I had used in business and personal development.

Then one day, I found myself thinking about fears in life—my fears now after delivering Kailani. I never imagined being an individual who would experience the loss of a baby. I mean, early in my pregnancy, I had all the thoughts about all the things that could go wrong. My mom would tell me not to worry and that I needed to stop thinking that way. Of course, I listened. As a result, I had not prepared for actually having to experience such a thing. Though I do not think it is possible to prepare one for such a soul shattering and heartbreaking experience.

I mean, leading up to this experience, my biggest fear in life was having loved ones in my life not knowing how I felt about them, should something happen to me. Then, all of a sudden, I was living the nightmare of having our baby die. Then it hit me, and I thought, What if Kailani's memory is forgotten? I mean, her life was so incredibly short and had such a significant impact on my life, Matt's life, and so many others. I felt absolutely devastated at the thought that when those who are part of her story die, her memory will go with them.

I couldn't let that happen. I needed a way to keep her memory alive, even after we die. I needed to share her story. Our story. Her memory. The grief. The heartache. How to carry it. How to find meaning. Most importantly, how her death resulted in something beautiful and purposeful. I needed to ensure her memory lived on.

I decided then, in that moment. I would share her story by writing a book. I didn't know how I was going to do it. I just knew it needed to be done. I had always felt like I would write a book one day, though I never thought the topic would be the loss of our baby and the grief that followed.

EMOTIONAL ROLLERCOASTER

Once my muscle tension decreased and the pain was gone, I started to feel the emotional weight of what Matt and I had just been through. The best way I can describe the second week post-delivery is that of a rollercoaster. I mean, the whole thing was a rollercoaster, though this second week was truly about me becoming more familiar with how I emotionally responded to grief and what that looked and felt like. It literally became a series of ups and downs as the seconds, minutes, hours, and days passed.

Admittedly, emotions are not something in which I am well versed. I have always been one to suppress my emotions and avoid showing them at all costs. Doing this made others perceive me to be cold and unsupportive at times. Though, from a positive standpoint, I feel that allowed me to take inspired action that was not driven by my emotions. I always felt that I was able to see things from a logical point of view. However, this approach had prevented me from truly healing and moving forward through many of my previous life challenges, and I was aware of this.

For the first time in my life, I began to allow myself to feel all the emotions. I felt angry, envious, guilty, depressed, sad, heartbroken, confused, overwhelmed, and so much more. And to be completely honest, the moment I caught myself feeling happy or relaxed, I felt angry and guilty with myself for feeling that way. How dare I feel that way? Our daughter died; I had no right to feel happiness ever again. I mean, grieving isn't about feeling happiness, joy, or fulfillment. I had a skewed concept of grief and what it was in those first weeks. I held the typical societal view on what grief was and was not. However, as I gave in to myself and my feelings, I began to reveal the truth behind grief.

As I thought about it more, I didn't want to hold onto those negative feelings. If my parents had gone through what Matt and I did, I would want them to focus on nothing but love, happiness, and fulfillment in their lives. So why is it that grief is viewed in such a negative light? Why is emotion considered taboo or a sign of weakness? Allowing ourselves to feel what we feel and express what we are feeling is healthy. It is part of the process of moving through our struggles and challenges, embracing them, and learning to carrying the weight of them with us.

Once I chose to embrace my emotions, something changed in me. Even my mom has come to describe me differently and views me as a softer and more approachable individual. Maybe this was part of my lesson and part of the knowledge and wisdom gained through this experience. Instead of avoiding my emotions, I decided to embrace them all. When I feel sadness, I allow the tears to take over, and I allow myself to feel the emotions with every part of my being. I allow myself to get lost in that moment. I allow myself to simply be, and I allow myself to be present. Most importantly, I allow and give myself the opportunity to heal.

And let me tell you, it is exhausting! Allowing myself to feel all these emotions is so incredibly draining. Initially, I struggled to accomplish anything in my day. I went to bed tired and woke up tired. I felt like I had nothing left me in.

I remember lying in bed one night with tears running down my face and onto Matt's chest as he held me. I honestly didn't think that my body could continue to keep up with the production of tears. I was convinced that I was going to end up completely dehydrated, as I didn't feel like I could replace my fluid loss at an adequate rate.

As I began to lean into my grief and embrace my emotions, I noticed a change. I noticed that my tears of heartache slowly began to shift to tears of love. Not only that, but my emotional turmoil began to settle. As the days passed, my emotional breakdowns started to occur less and less frequently. I was slowly moving away from being emotionally triggered by everything. Instead of feeling triggers that resulted in tears, I would experience triggers that brought on overwhelming amounts of love and gratitude.

One afternoon, Matt and I decided to take Gibson to the river. Matt felt it was a good opportunity to get me out of the house, as I really had not been going anywhere. Matt and I sat down in a sanded area in silence; my mind drifted. I began to think about a parallel life where Kailani was with us. I envisioned us in that spot with her at different stages of her growth. Imagining what could have been remains a challenge, though the memory of her also warms my heart and my soul. Matt interrupted my thoughts and asked what I was thinking about. I told him and asked what he was thinking. Turns out that he, too, was imagining the same thing.

In those first weeks and months, everything became a reminder of what could have been. Looking into the backyard would bring tears to both Matt and me, as we envisioned a yard full of toys, treehouses, and jungle gyms with her running around, Gibson following behind. When a child dies, everything becomes *what could have been . . .*

- One month, two months, three months old . . .
- First roll over, first crawl, first steps
- First solid foods, first full night's sleep
- First words, first haircut, first day of school
- First boyfriend, graduation, off to college
- Wedding days, grandchildren, great-grandchildren

Looking around at other families and their children is a constant reminder of what could have been, what would have been. And the saddest thing is that one in four pregnancies result in a loss. One in four. Interesting how pregnancy and infant loss has such a high rate, yet it is something that people rarely talk about. So, when I look at my family and friends with children, I know that some of them endured the heartache of a miscarriage, stillbirth, or infant loss prior to being where they are today. However, rarely do people speak about it because society does not allow, acknowledge, or encourage it. Instead, society wants to suppress it and hide it.

This experience brought a whole new perspective. I now felt so much more love and appreciation for the happy, healthy, strong, and resilient babies and children who are living in this world. Because twenty-five percent of them do not make it. Not only that, over time I did gain a patience I didn't have before. Now, I hear a child screaming and a mom looking so stressed out in the grocery store and find myself thinking, *What a blessing to be gifted that child.* Before I would have been annoyed with the screaming, just as the mother likely felt in those moments.

I wasn't expecting this shift. I was actually scared that this experience would make me bitter and resentful toward others with children. No, it's not fair that my baby didn't survive. Though I do not wish this on anyone and holding resentment and hate towards others does not help my healing. So I gave myself permission to approach these situations differently, because I do have a choice in how I respond in any scenario.

My best friend Tsarina, who wrote the poem "Sweet Mama," gave birth to her beautiful little man in June 2020. I had not yet met him or seen her since her delivery and the birth of her little man. We had been talking back and forth and finally made arrangements for a visit at the end of August.

When the day finally came and I was driving to her place, I honestly was thinking to myself, *Can you do this or is it going to turn you into an emotional train wreck?* I honestly didn't know. I did not know how I was going to react or feel when I finally saw them. I mean, she got her happily ever after, and I loved that. However, I was still going through my grief and trying to come to terms with the fact that I did not get what I signed up for. And honestly, I did not know how I was going to respond until I was in that moment. Sometimes the best way to figure out how we are going to be is to allow ourselves to experience the situation.

When I finally held him and saw the love between her and this sweet little boy, my heart filled. I am so incredibly happy that she gets to experience motherhood in a way that I one day hope to. And the most incredible thing was coming to understand and realize how impactful Kailani's death had been in her life, too.

I mean, we had planned to raise our children so they would grow up being best friends, just like the two of us. And now, that was gone. We were both heartbroken over it. It truly is amazing how life can take a sharp turn and have such a significant impact on those around us, in more ways than we realize.

It was not until this interaction that I began to shift my focus a little bit to observing how this impacted those around me. I mean, I know there were family and friends who shared our heartbreak through this experience, though there were so many others impacted too.

For example, a couple of months after Kailani's death, I learned that my experience of losing my baby girl helped others in my life be more present in the moment with their children. It allowed them to learn the value of patience and practice more of it. Because of Kailani's death, people started sharing with me how it changed their behaviours with their children and how they were becoming better parents because of it. We often take the small things for granted, and this was a means to remind people not to. Maybe this experience was not reserved for only me and Matt, but for others in our life as well.

And do not think for a second that I think it is fair. Because I don't. It is not fair that it took me losing my daughter for others to realize and appreciate what they have. However, that is what it has provided to some people. If it has made them a different and better person or parent because of it, well, then that is the beauty of it. I give myself permission to see this as a positive. There can be beauty even in the ugliest of situations. We may need to fight to find it and we may need to look in different places. Sometimes it is something external from us, whereas other times it could be something internal. Though once I opened my heart up to this, it changed my experience of grief.

WHO AM I,
NOW THAT YOU ARE GONE?

I wake up,
I lose my breath;
To be honest, I'd prefer death.

I laugh, I cry,
No one understands;
Life without you, is like drowning in quicksand.

My body aches,
My heart breaks;
I don't know how much more of this I can take.

So, I ask for a sign,
A way to connect;
You follow through, on my request.

A butterfly, A dragonfly
A feather or two.

It's your way of saying,
"Mommy, I am with you."

So, I keep pushing forward,
You keep sending me signs.

And I look forward to the day,
When we look into each other's eyes.

It is then you will see,
Who and what I've become.

All because you are my angel,
My gravity and sun.

IDENTITY CRISIS

Life post-Kailani has been completely overwhelming as I continue to navigate through my grief and write about this experience. I have felt absolutely everything there is to feel: happiness, sadness, love, hate, hope, despair, pain, euphoria, and everything in between. Yet, it was not until I had my second session with my counsellor that I could finally put a finger on what it was that I was experiencing in addition to my grief.

Yes, I was going through mourning and grieving. However, there was something deeper than that. When Kailani died, something changed within me, and I had not adequately identified what it was until recently. This entire experience changed me to the core. I mean, I knew that it would from the beginning. Though something was off, and I could not quite pinpoint what exactly it was.

It was not until my counsellor said it out loud. It was October 19, 2020, that I had finally figured it out with her help. When Kailani died, I lost my identity. The person I had worked so hard to create leading up to this experience was now gone; I didn't know who I was anymore.

I had always been one who was goal-oriented and career-driven. In my earlier years, I had not fully committed to the idea of being a mother in my lifetime. I had developed a success-driven self-identity that focused on building a legacy through a career. Then, when I became pregnant, I went through the process of changing my identity to one that included me being a role model and mother to a child, someone to look up to and someone who managed a family. However, I never anticipated or planned for the realities that I am now living.

Now I am a mother, without a living child. What does that mean? I have experienced an array of emotions, yet do not fully understand or feel that I am able to express all of them. And to put the cherry on top, the identity I developed while I was pregnant does not align with the reality I am living. Who the hell am I now that she is gone?

I had done a lot of work and personal development prior to my pregnancy around building my identity. I do believe that the key to a crisis situation is self. I must admit, I have been moving through this experience in a way that surprises many, including myself, and I attribute this to my growth mindset and dedication to always bettering myself.

In the hours that followed Kailani's death, I felt like everything would eventually be okay because I always figure things out. I told Kailani that we were going to be okay because I believe that it is through love and heartache that our souls develop. Through the most traumatic and most challenging experiences of our lives, we are given the opportunity to transform. As we learn in physics, for every action, there is an opposite and equal reaction. Meaning that with the tragic and the heartbreak can come beauty and gratitude. Though I believe we must be open to receiving and allowing this in our life. We also must be open to practising patience, as things do not happen overnight.

I recognize that I have the capacity to manage my behaviour and reactions throughout this experience. I also acknowledge that I am tasked with having to embark on a new journey of self-discovery as a result of this experience. As many individuals do, we start asking, "Who am I? What did I do wrong? Why me? How can I possibly live on?" following such challenging and life-changing events. Sadly, none of us are exempt from such hardships and adversities. We all have our battles to face. Although, I have found that by changing the questions I ask myself, I can change my life and how I experience it.

I changed "Who am I now that you are gone?" to "Who will I become?"

I changed "What did I do wrong?" to "What can I do moving forward?"

I changed "Why me?" to "What beauty will I create in my life in the future?"

I changed "How can I possibly continue living?" to "What would make you proud?"

I started asking myself some serious questions. Who am I, as a mother to a child who is not living? Who am I, recognizing that I am a grieving mother? My entire being has shifted, and I have not taken the time to explore what that truly means to me or who exactly I am now that she is not here.

I shared with my counsellor that I am scared of how my new self will manage in my old life. I went through this transformational experience, yet I still have to return to a career and routine I developed when I was a completely different person. I am scared that I am no longer the person I was before this experience. And because of it, I know that I will not be, do, or act the same way I did before this all happened. If I cannot be, do, or act like the previous me, might this have a negative impact on the life I have created for myself? Better question yet, is the life I am living the life I want to move forward with? Or do I want to change it? How do I want to change it?

Prior to this experience, I excelled in my work. I enjoyed the work that I was doing and took pride in how I managed certain tasks. However, I now question whether or not I want to continue in this line of work, given that my priorities have shifted. I recognize that I have a new perspective on life. Although, I have come to realize that this does not mean I cannot continue to excel in my "old" life. It simply means that I must re-evaluate whether or not my new identity aligns with the previous patterns, habits, and routines of my old identity. And if not, that is okay.

I remember something from a book I read last year by Maxwell Maltz that said something along the lines of, "our scars can either be a liability or an asset, though where we go from here is our responsibility." I took some time to reflect and think about this. I am no longer the same person that I was, but that does not have to be a negative thing. It simply means that I now have a new way of being and doing things, which does not mean that it is wrong.

I had become so conflicted over the question of "Who am I?" It is a question I had been working so hard to answer leading up to my pregnancy. I had done so much work around my identity prior to pregnancy and during pregnancy to prepare myself for how I would be, do, and act as a mother with a living child; however, I did not go through the process of preparing for the outcome of being a mother without a living child.

The reality is, though, that most people do not prepare themselves for worse case scenarios. Because honestly, that is depressing, and why would one want to focus on the negative? Matt and I literally won a golden ticket that no one wants, including us. In fact, the presumed diagnosis listed in the preliminary autopsy report does not even have an occurrence rate because there is such a limited number of cases reported worldwide (less than seventy-five). Our chances of winning the lotto are significantly higher, yet the likelihood of us actually winning the lotto is slim. Also, I do not buy a ticket, so that takes me out of the race.

However, our identity and how we be, do, and act is completely in our hands. That is up to us. It is our choice. As with all challenges in life, the best way to deal with them is by confronting them instead of avoiding them. At first, I was looking at the opportunity to explore what it was about my new identity that worried me. Then, I realized I needed to change my approach.

So I made a shift and started exploring how this experience improved and changed my sense of being. And guess what? There is always something positive in every situation. I said it. You can fight it and argue it until you are blue in the face. However, I have found that when an individual adopts a growth mindset, they are gifted new perspectives. I've listed some of the positives that resulted from this whole experience in previous chapters. They are there; it is just a matter of finding new perspectives and coming at it from a different angle. Sometimes the positive has nothing to do with me or my life. As heartbreaking and tragic as some might think my story is, it has been an inspiration for many. And that is beautiful. Not fair, but beautiful.

I am not going to go into great depth into my reflections and outline how I pushed through my identity crisis, although gaining new perspectives was a huge part of this process. Cultivating a growth mindset was a key factor for me.

To finish up this chapter, I will leave you with a couple of questions to reflect on, as they helped guide me in finding new perspectives.

- In what ways might you be underestimating yourself?
- In what ways might you be overestimating the adversity you are facing?
- Are you confronting your problems/fears, or avoiding them? Why?
- The way forward is through action; are you willing to receive feedback and correct your course as you move forward?
- Do you have an idea of who you want to be and how you want to act?
- Who do you want to be and how do you want to be remembered?

Remember, your brain and body functions are dependent on *you*. You control the machine. Trial and error are essential and may be the only way to gain answers to some of the questions we have in this life. For myself, the two questions that really helped me move forward with embracing this new life and a new identity are as follows:

- Who do I want to be when I see my little girl again?
- Would Kailani be proud of the person I am or the person I have transformed into because of our story together?

Remember, we all have the potential to create our reality. If you can imagine it, you can create it. Are you living your life based on who you *perceive* yourself to be, or who you *conceive* yourself to be? We are ever-evolving beings who can achieve whatever we set our minds to, even in the face of adversity. We all deserve happiness, regardless of what story we might be telling ourselves. Our loved ones would want us to be happy, they're cheering us on. So, I invite you to give yourself permission to move forward. I believe that Kailani would want me to be happy, and I believe that each and every one of our babies is wishing us a life of abundance, love, and happiness.

WHO I AM,
NOW THAT YOU ARE GONE

Strong, fierce and beautiful,
That is who you were to me.

If it wasn't for your guidance,
I would no longer be.

You guided me through it all,
both the good and bad.

Forever my little angel,
That pulled me from the quicksand.

I thank you for our story,
I thank you for your strength.

It is because of our story together,
my heart will always ache.

Regardless of the pain,
You help guide me through.

You taught me important life lessons,
You made me into somebody new.

Now I too am strong and fierce.
Just as my angel above.

No words will every express,
my gratitude and love.

Although I wish you were here,
I know it was meant to be.

Because without you watching over me,
I couldn't transform into this new me.

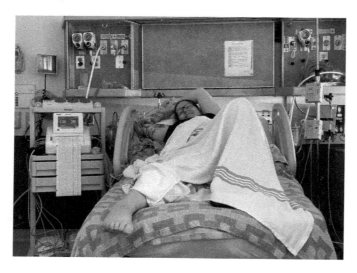

The picture Matt took when I suggested we begin documenting our journey. This was taken at the hospital that first examined me and relayed that my membranes had ruptured.
(July 20, 2020 at 11:19 a.m.)

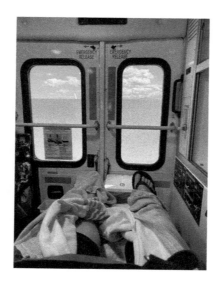

A picture taken in the back of the ambulance that was taking me to the airport to be lifted to Alberta. (July 20, 2020 at 2:32 a.m.)

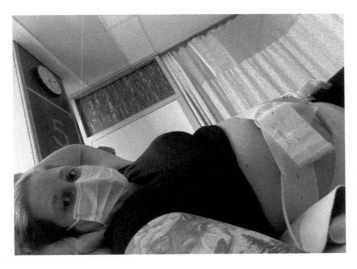

This was taken shortly after I arrived at the Foothills Hospital in Calgary while I received triage and was waiting for Matt to arrive (July 20, 2020 at 5:14 p.m.).

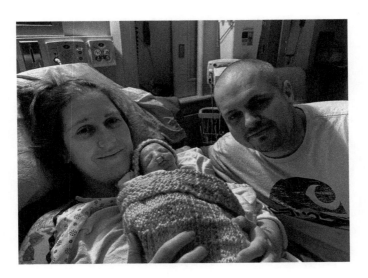

Our very first family photo, shortly following delivery. The nurses were absolutely amazing and helped us to capture these special moments that we will forever hold in our hearts.

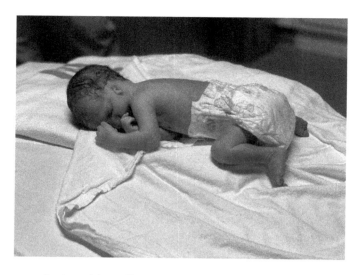

Our sweet baby girl, Kailani Mary. If I could go back and do it all over again, I would have spent more time examining every part of her. Although she looks big in the photos, she was only three pounds and twelve ounces of pure perfection.

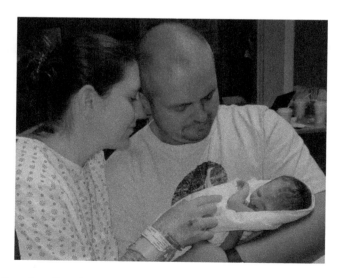

Another family photo. I treasure each and every one of these photos the nurses took and only wish there were hundreds more.

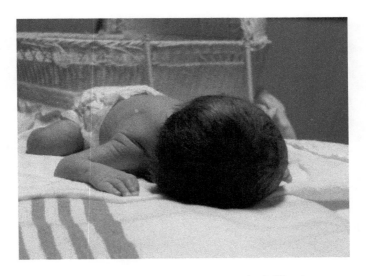

I just had to include her hair!!!! I mean, dark like her momma, though the top already had curls like her daddy. I can only imagine how long it would have been should she have been delivered full-term.

This photo was taken October 15, 2020. This was the first year that we became aware of and participated in the pregnancy and infant loss awareness day. Interestingly, if you google October 15, this does not automatically indicate the significance of this day. You must include pregnancy and infant loss (PAIL) for it to come up. Note: October is pregnancy and infant loss awareness month, although many websites and organizations do not acknowledge this, as their focus remains on breast cancer, SIDS, Rett syndrome, and autism.

PART 2

THE GOOD,
THE BAD, AND
THE UGLY OF GRIEF

KNOW THE DIFFERENCE

In my experience, people seem to think grief ends when mourning stops. Not only that, but there also appears to be this belief that grief must end. However, this is far from the truth. Sometimes our grief never leaves us, even after mourning is no longer evident. Because grief is the result of love. Without love, there wouldn't be grief.

For me, mourning had been a new experience as historically I did not make a habit of expressing my emotions. I admit, I had previously struggled with managing emotions and sharing them with others. When I started on my journey, it was important for me to understand that there is a difference between grieving and mourning. Take note that just because mourning is not evident in a person's life does not mean that they are not experiencing grief.

Mourning

As with everything in life, we all respond and react to the loss of a loved one differently. For many, the most immediate outward response to a loved one dying, which is seen by others, may be the act of crying or the expression of deep sadness. When we express feelings of grief in an outward fashion that can be observed by others, such as the act of crying, this is referred to as mourning.

The mourning period can fluctuate from person to person and may depend on the connection between the individual and the deceased. The mourning period may also depend on the specific spiritual or religious practices of an individual. There can be various ways in which one mourns, and it is not always an expression of emotion such as sadness or anger. For some individuals, expressions of mourning a loved one are done through wearing specific clothing or performing specific rituals. This can greatly differ based on the values, beliefs, religions, commitments, and cultures of individuals.

Grief

When a person in our life dies, there is an internal psychological and physiological response that occurs within our bodies. This internal response to bereavement is called grief and can include a variety of symptoms that may be physical, emotional, mental, and spiritual in nature. The reality is that grief can impact *every* aspect of our life.

Symptoms of grief might include:

- sadness
- numbness
- anger
- anxiety
- inflammation
- immune system suppression
- muscle aches
- headaches
- stomach pains and/or nausea/vomiting
- insomnia
- depression
- questioning one's religion or deity
- questioning one's life purpose
- isolation

This is not an extensive list, and individuals should note that symptoms of grief can vary from person to person. For an individual experiencing grief, it is important to recognize the different thoughts, feelings, and symptoms they are experiencing within their body. For those around us, it is essential to recognize that grievers' thoughts and feelings may not translate to an outward expression of mourning and grief. Therefore, it may be difficult to identify when a person is grieving. I feel, in this sense, this is where the saying "suffering in silence" might be an appropriate phrase to use.

Grief is complicated. To further complicate it, grief has different stages: acute, integrated, and complicated grief are the three I will discuss. Acute grief is what results immediately following the death of a loved one. Acute grief often feels like the death and loss of the individual is dominant and all-consuming in one's life. Over time, this may feel less dominating in life and usually transitions into what is called integrated grief.

The reality is that the thoughts and feelings we have for those who die will forever be present in our lives. However, when grief no longer dominates our life, we then transition into a state of integrated grief. Those who've experienced the death of a loved one can attest that we are left with a void within us. Unfortunately, this void is something that remains with us forever. When we transition into an integrated state of grief, we are able to continue pushing forward in our lives while we carry that void. We enter this stage once we truly allow grief and joy to be present within our lives.

Last, there is complicated grief. This form of grief follows acute grief and is the result of unresolved grief. Unresolved means that an individual has not been able to transition into a state of integrated grief. Complicated grief can occur when grief continues to consume and dominate one's life; it is the persistence and continuation of what individuals often see in the acute phases of grief for a prolonged period. Now, society tends to see this as being weeks or months after the loss. However, I am speaking of a much longer time frame, as grief is not something that one overcomes or gets over. I am speaking about those cases in which years have passed and there is still no light to the end of the tunnel, so to speak. I am talking about when our grief is all-consuming and has prevented us from moving forward in continuing to live a meaningful and fulfilling life. I am talking about when our grief has continued to conquer, and it feels all suffocating, all the time, and joy is non-existent. In such cases, it is important for individuals to speak to a health care provider or medical professional for additional support. More specially, one might consider speaking with someone who is familiar with grief and who can provide support and assistance with complicated grief.

Now, for those experiencing grief, know that it is okay to feel everything you are feeling, whatever that might look like for you. I also want to provide some reassurance that things will get better. Maybe not easier, though once I gave myself permission to welcome joy and laughter back into my life, it did get better. I am not going to say that time heals wounds, because time alone does not. The grief does not go away. However, it does get better over time in that we can become stronger in carrying our grief with us. I once heard an analogy about how it equates to going to the gym.

If we go to the gym consistently and perform specific movements with a certain amount of weight, over time, that weight will not feel as heavy. The weight does not change, though our ability to carry that weight changed.

Grief after the death of a baby does not disappear, though our ability to carry our grief moving forward can improve. It may take a long time, and this is not to say that every day will be easier or lighter; however, we do become stronger. Regardless of where you are at in your journey, acknowledge and honour where you are. Recognize and acknowledge that you do not need to get from A to B in a certain amount of time. This is your journey, and you will find what works for you. You will move through your grief at a pace that works for you and figure things out along the way. The reality is, there is no fixing grief. There is no eliminating grief. There is only figuring out what works for each of us, and what doesn't.

For some, it might be weeks, months, or years. Regardless of how long it takes, know this: it is okay to not be okay (as Megan Devine has written). Know that grief is a completely individualized experience, and there is no right or wrong way to experience mourning and grief. It actually took me some time to come to this realization and accept how I was mourning and grieving.

The expression of my emotions has always been something that I was not comfortable or familiar with. In the past, I would always suppress my emotions out of fear that it made me look a certain way to those around me. I developed the belief from an early age that emotions weren't tolerated and "big girls don't cry." I can actually pinpoint the situation in my life where this belief was developed: I was five years old.

For many years, I went through life without expressing how I felt. I would push down my emotions toward everything and tell myself to smarten up and be rational. Over time, what happened was I would have periods where I would completely break down and feel overpowered by my emotions. So much so, it got to the point where I thought I was having a panic attack. I had become so accustomed to not dealing with my emotions that I didn't know what they really felt like. Then, when they showed up, I would disengage and lose it because I didn't know what I was experiencing.

When I gave birth to Kailani and the nurse told me she no longer had a heartbeat, I didn't cry immediately. For quite some time, I felt guilty about this. However, this does not mean I wasn't hurting. I honestly was so wrapped up in just holding our little angel that the reality of things didn't really kick in. To look at her, she just looked so peaceful. It was like she was sleeping. I mean, I knew deep down that all that was left was her vessel; however, things didn't hit me hard until the nurse took her out of the room.

Having them wheel her bassinet away, with a blanket draped over her, is forever burned into my memories. I honestly don't think that any amount of time will lessen the heartache I feel when I relive that moment in my mind. In all honesty, it feels like I am dying and going through it all over again. My muscles tighten. I can't catch my breath.

I can't swallow. Parts of my body shake, and I have so much sadness in my heart that it feels like it is going to explode. The only way I've learned to overcome these feelings is by allowing myself to get lost in them; I simply let my emotions out and ride that wave.

I cry. I scream. I let my feelings be known, and I don't hold back. I cry as though it is July 25, 2020, and it is happening all over again. Because, in my mind, it is as real as the day it happened. Then the feelings begin to settle, and I can feel the weight begin to lift off my shoulders, slightly. By diving into my feelings and facing my reality, I release the hold it has on me, just a bit. Enough to move forward and continue living.

I no longer feel the need to scream. My muscles start to relax. I take a deep breath and allow my lungs to fill. The tears start to slow. Then I give myself permission and choose to move forward. I got through that moment. That is another moment that I survived. Now, what do I do? I give myself permission to put one foot in front of the other, and I make another choice, another decision to continue to live.

Now, these breakdowns can happen once a day or ten times a day. They show up randomly and without a moment's notice. However, what I have noticed is that over time, the frequency of these break-downs has decreased. The key has been that each time they come up, I allow myself to go through the motions and feel them. I ride that wave as I know it is part of my journey and part of my healing.

I choose to heal, and I choose to focus my experience on the love that was created. I remind myself that I am not easily broken. I am Kailani's mother, and I will live on to share her story with the world. And honestly, not every situation can be transformative in a positive way, though I do believe there is beauty to be found in every situation. However, I recognize that I have a choice in how I respond and react. And I give myself permission to see this as a beautiful experience. Never would I trade this for a life without my baby girl.

Once I started allowing myself to truly feel and express my grief, I was able to navigate through it more easily and learn ways to integrate it into my life. I was able to see that I was not a victim of my circum-stance. I believed and gave myself permission to create something beautiful from this. I had to do the work to make this so and needed to be open to accepting the challenge. I recognized this was not going to be an easy task, especially given the various triggers that could bring my grief to surface.

If you find yourself experiencing such pain as I have, I invite you to feel and face the pain. Get lost in the pain and be present in your heartache. Do the work of being emotional and feeling it all. Though, give yourself permission to heal. Give yourself permission to move forward *with* your mourning and your grief. Because, honestly, things don't get easier right away. In fact, quite the opposite, in my experience. Things got worse before they began to get better, because what followed was a long list of triggering moments and events that set me off. If I allow it, these events and situations can become all-consuming, tear me down, and set me back. They could keep me stuck in my grief and prevent me from moving forward in my healing. However, I give myself permission and I invite others to do the same. Make a commitment to heal. Make the decision to carry your grief with you while you move forward in this life.

TRIGGERS OF GRIEF AND MOURNING

The afternoon of July 25, 2020, was my first introduction to what was to follow in the coming weeks and months of my grief. For those who are new to grief, this is a warning. There are so many different things that can trigger your grief and trigger the memories of your loved one. Be further warned, this can come with zero warning and at the most inconvenient time.

These triggers can present in different ways. They may be sounds, tastes, sights, or experiences. There is no limit on what these might look like and each has the potential to trigger or heighten our mourning and grief. These, of course, are different for everyone and are not something that we all experience. However, it is important to recognize and acknowledge these. The following are a few examples of the triggers I've experienced. When I am faced with triggers, I ask myself, *Is my reaction or response to these triggers a means for me to avoid or suppress my grief, or are they a means to support me in my healing?*

Auditory Triggers

The sound of a baby crying gets me every time. I don't think that there will ever be a point in my life when I hear a baby cry and am not triggered. After delivering Kailani and being on the labour and delivery ward, I became resentful toward the other labouring individuals and their crying babies. I never got to hear Kailani's cry and often wonder what she would have sounded like. Every time I hear a baby cry, it takes me back to the seconds after I delivered my sweet baby girl. In these moments, I have to actively focus my perspective and thoughts on how beautiful and calming the sound of my own baby girl would have been. Because, if I allow for it, my mind can start a downward spiral, building resentment and frustration and beginning a pity party that will extend for weeks and months. I do not want to live like this. Plus, crying babies are something I must face almost daily.

I work in healthcare and oversee an area that deals with babies. The reality is this may always be a trigger for me, though I cannot hide from it, nor do I want to. So I had to change my perspective and focus my mindset on something productive. For me, that is the thought and wondering of how Kailani's cry would have sounded.

Anytime I find myself in a situation where I am triggered, I remind myself of this: I do have control over what I allow in my life. I have a choice in how I can respond to such situations. I am not saying it is easy and there are times when grief overpowers me, and I allow my emotions of resentment and frustration to triumph. However, I continue to work toward changing this response to something that allows me to move forward with my grief. I have reminders in my notebooks, my agenda, my phone, etc. Everywhere and anywhere that I may see it or need easy access to this reminder.

Another auditory trigger for me is certain songs. There are specific songs that trigger the memories and emotions of this whole experience. For example, when I woke up on July 26, 2020, from my nap in the vehicle on the drive home, the song "I Hope" by Gabby Barrett and Charlie Puth was playing. At that time, I was not really paying attention to the lyrics, as I was more focused on the time—4:44 p.m., as I shared previously. However, the song came on again as we got closer to home, and I began to listen to the lyrics. Then I started to cry.

During the first couple weeks after Kailani died, I listened to this song over and over again. Although the lyrics are talking about cheating girlfriends/boyfriends, I viewed the song differently and felt like it applied to my life so accurately. Discovering I was pregnant and growing our little girl in my body brought so much joy to me. Matt and I were entering into the commitment of parenthood, and when she died, it was like I had been cheated by life. I was so incredibly angry.

It took a few months for me to not break down and cry every time I heard this song. There would be days when I would be driving and this song would come on the radio, then I would have to pull over because I was crying so hard. Yes, although I could have changed the station, I knew that the reason for me doing this was to avoid these thoughts and feelings. As much as I didn't want to face them, I knew that I needed to let these emotions out and face these triggers to allow healing to take place.

Another song that gets me every time is "I'll Never Love Again" by Lady Gaga and Bradley Cooper. My ability to change the storyline of almost any song into one that relates to the death of my daughter is astonishing. That, or I am reminded of when I was pregnant listening to a song, or I imagine how, if she would have lived, Kailani would be listening to it with me in that moment.

For many individuals, specific songs are a trigger to their grief. Some, like me, choose to listen to the song, whereas others may choose not to. There is no right or wrong way to do grief. Though, I ask that individuals consider and acknowledge that these triggers might be part of the grieving journey. Also know that you are not alone in this experience.

Explore your triggers and get to know them. Decide if it is something that you feel you need to avoid or something that you will face, as some of these might aid in the healing process.

Visual Triggers

As I shared previously, when I first came home from the hospital, my mom had moved all the baby stuff into the nursery and placed a sheet over the crib—the crib that Matt and I had built for Kailani. For many grieving parents, entering the nursery can be one of the most challenging things following the death of their baby.

Initially, I thought that going into that room was going to break me. I honestly was not sure how I would ever be able to face going in there again. Though, after a short period, I came to feel that the nursery is a place where I feel connected to Kailani, even though she had never been in that room.

Everything in the room was selected or made for our baby, our daughter, Kailani. Because she was early, we never completely finished the nursery. Though now, more than ever, I feel that I want it done so I can sit in there and be with all the things gifted, purchased, and made for our angel. So much love has filled that room. I just want to sit in there and absorb it all. Again, overcoming this obstacle had a lot to do with my mindset. Don't get me wrong; there are times when I go in there and bawl. Though I recognize it is the experience of allowing my pain and heartache to be present that allows me to move forward in my grief.

Other visual triggers include pictures, movies, books, baby items, clothing, etc. There really is no limit to what may pose as a visual trigger and it varies from one person to the next. These visual triggers can also come up anywhere. At home, a friend's house, family member's house, a store, social media, etc. For me, I knew that these were always going to be a reminder. Therefore, why avoid something that eventually I am going to have to face? However, I admit that there were things I could control and things I could not. So, I took every opportunity to take control where I could when I felt that it wouldn't slow my healing.

For some, avoiding any visual triggers or items that are a reminder of their loved one is a way to cope with and, in some cases, avoid their grief. For myself, I found it to be much more difficult to not have these items around me. To support my grief journey, I needed to allow these items to be present in my life. For this reason, I have multiple items that represent and honour our daughter throughout our home. Some are evident to others, whereas some items people wouldn't be able to make a connection or even notice them.

Examples include her urn, plants, paintings, macramé, pins, stones, stuffed animals, jewellery, and books. There is a painting I did of a sunset in my kitchen—I painted it a couple of weeks before I delivered Kailani. I was playing with the paint and did not like the painting, though now I cherish this item. In my bathroom is a decorative orchid; on the leaf, I attached an angel pin that I received as a gift following Kailani's death.

For me, having these visual triggers surrounding me has been essential in my healing. It allows me to feel more connected to my baby girl and can present as a conversation starter; and I love talking about my daughter. Others might find this creates strong feelings of grief and does not contribute to their healing, which is respect-worthy and perfectly okay. Again, everyone is different and works through their grief in their own unique way.

Developing New Fears

Now, I know this may sound a bit strange; however, what I have noticed is that following the loss of a child, many individuals start to develop different fears. I was definitely one of these people. For example, I became fearful of Kailani's memory being lost.

I felt very ashamed and embarrassed about my fears when they started to come about. I didn't talk about them with anyone until a couple of months after they developed. In addition to having Kailani's memory lost, my biggest fear was leaving my daughter's urn in the house while I wasn't there. I was absolutely terrified and convinced that some random person was going to break into our home and steal her urn. I am not even joking. Leaving the house created so much anxiety for me because of this fear.

For the first couple months, I brought her urn with me everywhere throughout the house. When I went to bed at night, she would be on my nightstand. When I woke up, she would come and have coffee with me on the deck. I literally took my baby's urn with me everywhere in the house—she didn't leave my sight. The one thing that prevented me from taking her with me out of the home was that I was scared of her urn getting damaged or stolen—go figure.

Over time, this fear subsided. What helped was having jewellery that I wore daily that were reminders of her. This way, I felt like she was with me everywhere I went. Matt and I are committed to having jewellery made that contains her remains, and I think that will further lessen my fear and anxiety. The other thing that helped lessen my fears was to talk about them. After about three months, I discovered that I wasn't crazy and that other people experienced similar thoughts. Once this happened, I felt more comfortable talking about it. Therefore, do not bottle it up; talk about it. You are not alone. We all seem to think that we are until one of us opens up, and then others come forward as they, too, feel the same way.

Body Image

Now I want to touch briefly on a trigger that many grieving individuals who have miscarried, experienced stillbirth, or had a neonatal loss experience. Pregnancy has a significant impact on our bodies and, unfortunately, our bodies don't just bounce back to the way they looked pre-pregnancy. The reality is our bodies do not know that our babies have died. These changes can be a constant reminder of what we are missing.

I have always struggled with my body image and my weight. When I became pregnant, I had to actively tell myself that it was okay that I was gaining weight because it was healthy and needed to support the growth and development of our baby. It took some time to be okay with the changes my body was undergoing. And here's the thing: many individuals, including other parents, often tell us, "It is worth it in the end." However, for us, we didn't get the "worth it" part of the deal; we no longer have our babies.

Once I delivered Kailani and didn't get to bring her home, I expected my body to go back to the pre-pregnancy body I had before. I was no longer pregnant, and I did not get my baby. Therefore, I didn't feel like my body should be and look the way it did. It did not do its job, so it had no right to experience all the post-pregnancy things that a body goes through. I mean, I knew that my body wouldn't just bounce back, though it didn't change how I felt or my unrealistic expectations at that time.

I was so annoyed and angry with my body. Then, during about week three post-delivery, I started to notice my actions and thoughts toward my body. I started to question my body. Did my body and my genetic make-up contribute to the result and this reality? Was this result because of my history of obesity and eating disorders? Maybe it is because I had gastric bypass when I was younger, and my body was not giving my baby the nutrition it needed? Did I do this? Did my actions toward myself and toward my body result in the death of our baby? Well, as you can imagine, those thoughts can send a person on a downward spiral.

I started to resent my body. If you are experiencing pregnancy loss or infant death and are feeling resentment toward your body, know that you are not alone in this. Others have felt and thought this way. I have felt this way. Our bodies have gone through some major transformations. It takes time to move through these feelings.

I had a conversation with someone who said she often wonders, what if she would have quit smoking, stopped drinking, eaten healthier, and exercised earlier in her pregnancy. She thought maybe the results would have been different for her. Funny thing is, I thought the same thing, though I was on the complete opposite end of the spectrum.

Maybe if I had not done everything by the book, I would have Kailani here today.

I see many individuals who have drank, smoked, and lived very unhealthy lifestyles while pregnant and then gave birth to a perfectly healthy baby. Yet, there are also those who do not. I followed almost everything in the book. I didn't drink. I didn't smoke. I didn't push myself during exercise; I listened to my body. I made better food choices. I quit drinking a pot of coffee in the morning; I quit coffee altogether. I eliminated carbonated drinks for the first couple trimesters then limited myself later on. I gave up things, as I was certain that this would ensure I had a healthy baby. Yet, here we are.

There is no guarantee. Statistics are one in four for *every pregnancy*. Just so happens, we are that one, and it sucks. We cannot change this reality and know this: it is not your fault. Moving forward is not easy, although cultivating the *belief* that I could not change the outcome and that I would survive this, helped me significantly. I give myself permission to *believe* that nothing would have changed the outcome. And I believe this because any other thought would drive me insane and pull me into a deep and dark depression.

Focusing and living in a world of what if, should have, and could have is not going to change my reality. I cannot change the past, though I can choose to develop a belief system that supports me in the present and further sets me up for happiness to exist in my life moving forward.

I am not going to lie. Changing my thoughts and feelings toward my body was not easy. It takes time and a lot of effort. Do not expect to push through it quickly or seamlessly. Though what helped me was to change the narrative that I told myself. What do I mean by this?

Instead of me saying that my body "did not" do this, my body "could not" do that, I changed how I talked to myself. Instead, I started focusing on what my body did provide. Because without my body, and without your body, our babies would not have existed at all. And as much as it breaks my heart and pains my soul to the core that I do not have Kailani here with me, I would much rather have this version of her than no version at all. I am quite certain that the majority of parents who have experienced pregnancy and infant loss (PAIL) would feel and say the same thing.

Therefore, I invite you to give yourself permission to change the narrative and maybe even your beliefs. Because, again, statistics are one in four; statistics alone are working against us. It is not fair, though this is our reality.

I am doing what I can to get answers as to why this happened. We opted to get an autopsy and genetic test done to see if the outcome was due to our make-up or not. Fortunately, or unfortunately, the tests did not reveal anything of significance. Regardless, Matt and I cannot change the cards that we were dealt. So, instead of holding onto the negativity and pulling myself down by focusing on the what-ifs of the past, I decided to focus on the what-ifs of the future.

What if when I die, I am met with my baby girl, and she says to me, "Mom, what the hell did you do with your life?! Why did you waste it? Why did you allow depression to take over? Why did you not take care of your health and wellness? Why did you allow my death to consume you and derail your life?"

Personally, if I was met with my daughter and she told me she was disappointed in me, that would be unbearable. To say I am a mess now, compared to what I would be in that situation . . . well, let's just say this is rainbows and butterflies because the last thing I would ever want is my daughter to be disappointed in me or who I am. I want my daughter to be proud of me and proud that I am her mom.

I give myself permission to honour my baby girl through my health and wellness. I honour my baby girl by taking every opportunity to take care of myself. I take every opportunity to be and do better, to honour Kailani. And, over time, I no longer was doing it just for Kailani; I was doing it for me too. Sometimes we have to allow the belief of others to lift us up and carry us forward until we begin to believe in ourselves. Therefore, find the people who believe you can and hold onto their belief in you.

As time has passed, I've come to love and appreciate my body for carrying our baby girl for the length of time that it did. Although our baby girl didn't survive, there is no part of me that wishes I had not gone through this experience. I love that I have her in my heart and in my memories. I love every experience that she has brought to me. Though my wish would be for her to have lived a long and healthy life, I would prefer this outcome versus not having her at all. And, yes, I am going to continue to say this over and over again because I believe that others feel this way too or will develop this belief over time.

Now, with that said, once I focused on my health as a way to honour my daughter, I was able to motivate myself to get back into a fitness routine. It is not easy, and many parents that I have connected with have said they don't have the energy, they feel depressed, and I totally get it.

Exercising, on a good day, is not something I overly enjoy doing. No lie, November 7, 2020, I put on some music and started dancing to try to get myself motivated. Well, that ended up with me on the floor, crying and screaming. So, I cried and I screamed. Then I got up again, started dancing, and pushed myself to complete the workout. How did I get this done? Well, I focused on the belief that my daughter holds a belief in me, even when I want nothing more than to give up. So in these moments, I leverage and lean on my daughter for strength. Guess what? After getting the workout done, I felt so much better.

For grieving individuals who are struggling with body image, working out can not only help with getting that kind-of pre-pregnancy body back, but it can also help in so many other ways. It can help one through grieving, and decrease the risk of depression, as it has a significant impact on our moods and the hormones our body produces.

Be open to exploring what is available. Do you have a friend or acquaintance who is a personal trainer or an online fitness coach? I am sure most of us know at least one person that is into fitness. I invite individuals to reach out to them and give it a go. Maybe find another mother/father/individual who has experienced something similar and support one another? There are tons of parents online to connect with. As per a post I saw a while back, the best time to focus on our health was yesterday. Thirty minutes is all it takes, and it can change your life in more ways than one might think.

Appearances

I want to touch on appearances for a brief moment. To all supporters, I might suggest avoiding making comments on how great or how terrible someone looks following the death of a loved one.

I've had people tell me that I am looking "good . . . considering." Now, this typically has happened when I have had to run out to the grocery store or do an errand. In all honesty, some days, it takes every ounce of energy I have to look "presentable" in the public eye. The reality is that I may have spent the past three hours leading up to that moment bawling my eyes out. In these moments, I might suggest avoiding discussion around one's appearance and simply ask how they are doing and apply the appropriate listening skills discussed previously. I might also invite individuals to consider where they are. Asking someone how they are doing, especially in a place like a grocery store, may not be the best setting. In such cases it might be best to tell them you are thinking of them and consider following up with the person in a different setting.

Also, for those who are grieving, you do not need to feel bad or apologize for how you look or for breaking down in aisle five because that is where they carry the baby food. You are allowed to feel like crap and look like you're having the most miserable time of your life. Just know that you are not alone and that I, too, feel this pain and have cried in many stores. Together, we hurt and sadly there is a long list of us who have bawled in aisle five. Speaking of grocery stores, I also have quite a few taste triggers.

Taste Triggers

Now, for me, this was more so due to having specific cravings while pregnant with Kailani. For example, in the first two trimesters of my pregnancy, I constantly craved sour candies. More specifically, sour keys. So now, anytime I have a sour candy, it makes me think of my pregnancy, and I go through an entire evaluation of what I did when I was pregnant (that what-if mindset starts to creep in, and I have to be careful that it does not take me down a rabbit hole). Also, watermelon and cantaloupe have the same effect. For my first trimester, I had to go vegetarian, as all meat made me sick. I constantly craved watermelon and cantaloupe. For as much watermelon and cantaloupe that I ate, I am surprised that I still enjoy it today.

In short, there are so many different things that can trigger the memories of our losses and resurface or heighten our grief. It is important to recognize that these triggers are real and may continue to be a challenge moving forward through our grief. Give yourself permission to feel this grief when it surfaces. The weight of the grief will lessen over time, although it will never be gone. By allowing ourselves the ability and capacity to live with both joy and grief in our lives, we allow ourselves to embrace these experiences, build our resilience, and move into a state of integrated grief.

Now I quickly want to touch on a subject that I became familiar with shortly after the death of Kailani. This is something called grief comparison, and it drives me absolutely crazy.

Grief Comparison

Grief is not a competition. Read that again. Jane's loss of her father is not any easier or more challenging in comparison to the loss of my daughter. Regardless, people seem to think and treat others differently, depending on who dies in a person's life. The label a person holds in their life does not dictate how they might mourn and grieve their death. Now, why do I say this?

It is simple. Grief is a completely subjective experience. As I've mentioned previously, the intensity and type of grief that a person experiences will change, depending on the connection and depth of the relationship held with the individual who has died. For example, I've had individuals share their story of having a miscarriage early in their pregnancy and say that they know it's nothing in comparison to what I've gone through. Here's the thing: our situations are different, and I cannot say that my grief is greater than theirs because our experiences are so incredibly different. Not only that, others should not feel the need to lessen their experience in comparison to my own. Both situations are heartbreaking. Loss is incredibly difficult.

Grief is grief. Yes, more often than not, when it comes to pregnancy or infant loss, this can be the most challenging experience a person has ever had to live through in their life. But this does not mean that I get to devalue another and say that the death of a distant relative does not compare. Because one, we all experience grief and loss differently, and two, grief is not a competition.

For those who've experienced a miscarriage or infant death, they might say that it was the most painful thing they have ever experienced. Yet, for someone else, the most painful experience they might have is from the death of a parent or sibling. Grief is not a means to compare who has more pain or worse pain. Though, we must recognize that neither party can fully understand the pain and the grief of the other because it is a completely subjective experience. Honour and respect that the death of any loved one is a painful experience—period.

On the other hand, I've also seen grief compared between grieving parents. There seems to be this belief that if a person carried their baby longer or a child lived longer than someone else's, that time somehow translates to it hurting more. So, I need to stop and ask, why is it a competition? Grief is not some game where we keep score. No one is winning here. Stop comparing.

We cannot compare our pain. All grieving individuals may experience emotional, physical, and spiritual pain, though do so very differently. It sucks any which way you look at it. And at the end of the day, for many individuals, the grief they are experiencing is the most difficult thing they have ever lived through. Everyone will experience and manage it differently.

At no point in time should we ever line people up and start comparing and ranking who has the worst-case scenario. Because honestly, the way in which our brains operate and how society has created a competitive system, most people will fight to be first, and it will be ugly.

Instead, let's honour and accept that we all manage and experience our grief differently. We all have varying capacities to manage and endure such pain and heartache. On any given day, our resilience changes. Our ability to manage and cope changes. So, for those who have ever been judged, rejected, or shamed, I invite you to choose understanding, acceptance, and compassion. No one has the right to judge another person. By eliminating judgments, we support healing, spread love, and build our relationships. Truthfully, this is needed even more so during times of grief.

Family and Friends

Unfortunately, there is the possibility that we may not receive the type of empathy and support we were anticipating from family and friends and this can heighten our grieving experience and strain our relationships. Now, if you feel like maybe you are someone who falls into this category, I want to congratulate you. Why, do you ask? Recognition is the first step, and if you are reading these pages, then it means that you care and are willing to learn a new way to support those around you. I hope that you find the chapters that follow helpful in taking on a supporter role.

For grieving individuals who come across family and friends who do not support them in their grief or understand what they are feeling, I know that this can be very difficult. Having supportive individuals in my life while I navigate through this journey has been essential to my health and healing. Unfortunately, as with many areas of our lives, if we are not receiving the support we need from certain individuals, we may need to consider finding that support elsewhere.

Having others in my life who have been or are going through a similar situations of PAIL has provided a different level of comfort than what family and friends can offer. There is a certain level of knowledge and wisdom that is offered by these individuals, which translates into a different kind of support and guidance. Also, when I am talking about my experience with others who have gone through the death of a child, I find myself sharing more. They understand me. There is zero judgment—just full acceptance and support. Therefore, I invite others who might be going through PAIL to be open to discovering different resources and methods of communicating to connect with others. The reality is that sometimes our immediate family and friends may not be our first choice on the go-to list for support and that is okay. Each of us needs to do what is best for our health and healing.

I have also found that there are times when I have had to restrict interactions with those who are not supportive in my grieving and healing. I am not saying we must cut people out of our lives completely; though if they are not contributing to our health and wellness, I might suggest that it is time to find a new group of supporters. Do not feel guilty for this. Again, you do what you need to support your grieving and healing process.

Relationships with Significant Others

A CNN reporter wrote an article in 2010 about the statistics found on the separation rates of couples who've experienced a miscarriage or stillbirth. At that time, it was reported that couples who experienced a miscarriage were twenty-two percent more likely to separate, and those who had experienced a stillbirth were forty percent more likely to separate. Those are high numbers. So, I want to take a moment to discuss grief and how it can impact our relationships and possible ways we can support our relationships during periods of grieving.

For many partners, they genuinely want to support and comfort their loved one in any way that they can. This often is the same for individuals going through shared grief. The challenge I've faced is that when there is a significant loss, especially that of a child, it changes a person's soul. That isn't to say that this is a bad thing; however, we need to prepare for and understand that our loved one may never be the same. And this can be the same for our partners. For many, this means that we are entering a new chapter of our relationship as individuals are no longer the same people we knew before. Now I am not a relationship expert, though the below methods are what have helped me following the death of our sweet baby girl Kailani.

When we are in our most acute stages of grief, our emotions can be heightened. This may, in turn, result in expressions of anger, resentment, regret, sadness, or other emotions. Everyone's experience is different. Part of the challenge here is when we go through the loss of a pregnancy or infant, our significant other can sometimes present as a frequent reminder of the experience and/or the loss. I mean, you created this life and this child together. Now this loss is changing one or both of you, significantly.

It can be challenging to watch the individual we love change so drastically and hurt so deeply. One of the most beneficial things we can do is practice listening and understanding. When it is difficult to look at your partner, husband, or wife because they are a constant reminder, this is something that needs to be discussed. Especially if you want the relationship to work. If you find it difficult to talk to your significant other, I invite individuals to seek appropriate support, as communication is key.

There are several approaches that couples and individuals can take to support one another. For me, recognizing and acknowledging that my husband's experience was different than mine and being respectful of this was essential. Furthermore, approaching these conversations about our grief *without* judgment was required.

Often, men cope and manage their grief very differently than women do, as men and women are often raised to think and act differently within society. Regardless of sex, our values, beliefs, role models, and society can have a significant impact how one might express or experience grief. Prior to this experience, I would have identified as someone who did not embrace or express my emotions with others. I would beat the crap out of my emotions and suppress them because I was brought up with the belief that "big girls don't cry."

Though, as a result of this experience, I cry a lot. I no longer stop to think or care about where or when my tears show up. There are days where I feel like I am so completely dehydrated that I could not possibly create another tear for a least a week. Yet, Matt does not show the same kind of outward expression of emotion as he compartmentalizes, as he calls it.

I used to be able to do that. Though, with this experience, I do not feel that I can suppress or file away any part of what I think or feel. Suppressing and hiding my thoughts and emotions is actually the last thing I want to do. I want Kailani's memory to be constant in my life because she is not gone, nor will she ever be gone. She lives on through my memory, through the way her existence has changed me and how her life has impacted those around me. And part of me placed an expectation that Matt should want to feel and do the same.

However, Matt compartmentalizes, which is his way of coping. He seems to think that this also translates to him being strong for me. I used to think that by not showing my emotions that I was being strong, too, though I have come to a new understanding of strength through this all. And though I wish he would give up this approach, I respect that this is his way to manage and cope with his grief. He knows that I am here for him, and I have told him that he does not need to be strong for me. I am strong for myself. Regardless, he is set in his beliefs, and I honour, respect, and accept that. I cannot expect him to change, just as he cannot expect me to change the way I process and have been moving through this experience.

Also, something I noticed is that Matt does not mention our little girl very often—to me. I am not even sure he notices this; maybe he does. Or maybe he does not feel the need to bring her up because I talk about her quite frequently, without cueing from him. He doesn't typically say much; he just listens. I am very grateful that he listens, though I really wanted to know what goes on inside his head. Early in the experience I was desperate to know that this had changed his life too and I wanted to know how it had changed his life.

We went through the death of our daughter, and it changed my world. It changed the way I feel, the way I think, everything about me. It changed me to the core and my state of being. Yet, for him, it would appear on the surface that he just jumped back to his old way of life. He didn't appear to be going through a change in his identity like I had experienced. However, maybe he was. I couldn't tell. Trying to read his mind and guess at what was happening for him did not get me anywhere. I had to ask.

It took some probing and a little bit of time to pass before I discovered he had been talking about our daughter. Quite a bit, actually; when he was at work. After he disclosed this, there would be days when he would come home and tell me that a client he was working with that day experienced a miscarriage or infant loss.

To be completely honest, at first, I was hurt because I felt like maybe he did not trust me or feel comfortable talking to me about it. Though, over time, I came to understand that this was not the case. It was simply his way to manage and cope. For me, knowing that he was having these conversations with others about our daughter made me feel more at ease because he was not bottling it all up and was connecting with others.

My point is, if I hadn't asked him directly, I would have likely continued to feel like I was the only one impacted on a larger scale and felt completely alone. I wouldn't have discovered that he was having conversations to support him in his healing journey.

There might be times when we may not understand why a person is doing what they are doing in times of grief, though I invite individuals to take the time to try to see it from the other person's perspective. We may never fully understand where they are coming from or why they choose to cope a certain way. However, the best thing we can do is simply support them if it is helping them through their grief; that is, if it is not causing harm to themself or others. I truly believe that relationships are about giving and receiving, while finding a balance to support one another and both individuals' needs. Though I recognize that this can be challenging when it's a one-way street.

In situations where one individual wants to discuss the experience and the other does not, the first step I found was to recognize and respect where each individual is at in their grieving journey. If your significant other wants to talk about the experience and you feel you are able to provide that space to listen, then absolutely by all means, do so. This is exactly what Matt did for me, though he didn't often talk about his experience or his feelings.

However, allowing your significant other the opportunity to talk about it may be part of what they need to move through their grief. Though if you are not able to provide a listening space, that is okay too. It truly is about partnership in these challenging times and finding ways to support one another, while also recognizing and honouring that what one person may need may not be what the other needs. In these cases, the key is to communicate and determine how to support each other in your grief experiences.

So, how do you know what a person needs? Be open to having the conversation. Communication is key in any relationship. Do not expect that your husband/wife/partner can read your mind and can anticipate what you need. If there is something that you would like them to do, have that conversation. The goal is to work together. It is a partnership. You may not understand why your partner/husband/wife is doing what they are doing in their grief, though the best thing we can do is provide support and aim to understand. Be open to having conversations and to listening. Maybe be open to trying new methods to work through grief and this experience together. Everyone's experience is different. Though, by allowing ourselves to work together, maybe we can beat the odds. I mean twenty-two and forty percent, that is huge.

Now, to be completely upfront, these types of conversations are not always easy, especially if you are experiencing emotions such as anger and resentment toward your significant other. I invite individuals to remember that you are in this together and are both hurting. You both experienced this loss and this pain. I can't imagine trying to work through this experience without leaning on my husband. Therefore, if couples are finding it challenging to connect and have a conversation, it may be easier to have a neutral third party to facilitate these. Yes, I am going to say it, and I know there will be many eye rolls, heavy exhales, flips of the pages, and maybe even shutting of the book. I do not care. If you want to move through your grief, remember:

1. Give yourself permission to grieve
2. Take what works and leave what does not

With that said, I found it extremely helpful throughout my experience to seek and receive professional support. Now, I found connecting with someone who is experienced in working with grieving families and PAIL to be key. However, if you are someone who has built a strong relationship with a healthcare professional that you find supportive, you may opt to stick with them. It is completely up to you.

Counselling/Coaching

Before making a concrete decision to refuse the aid of professional support, let me just say this. Seeking professional support does not translate into being a failure, or that you are weak, crazy, or whatever other misconception or stigma that are out there. The truth is, most people who are extremely successful in business, relationships, finance, etc., have often received some type of counselling, coaching, or mentorship support.

Not only that, many individuals who've experienced the death of a child and were initially reluctant to seek professional support now recommend it. When someone asks for advice on what actions to take to support their relationship or marriage following the death of a child, the responses from others who've been there have included: seek professional support, communicate, listen to one another, and compromise.

Now, when I say seek professional support, do not feel obligated to stick with the first person that you are referred to. You really do need to find someone who is the right fit for you. In my life, I've seen about half a dozen counsellors and have also had different business mentors along the way. Yes, I am someone who seeks support when I need it, and I feel no shame because it got me to where I am today.

When I was a teenager, I suffered from severe depression and suicidal ideation. Then going into young adulthood, I started to experience a lot of anxiety due to my body image. Just prior to my PAIL experience, I sought support for anxiety related to my work, which turned into exploring my need to control every aspect of my life and my obsessive-compulsive disorder. Yes, my name is LaCara and I like to have control over everything. PAIL definitely eliminated any control I previously felt I had in my life.

During my efforts to find a counsellor to help with my work-related anxiety, it took three different people before I found a good fit. The first counsellor actually turned the conversation around completely, and we spent the hour talking about her age, what she was experiencing in life, and the relationship she had with her mother. I ended up taking on the counselling role, which was not something I wanted or needed at that time. Regardless, sometimes we do not jive with certain individuals, and that is okay. It might take some time to find the right fit; just know there is someone out there who will meet your needs.

With Kailani and my neonatal experience, it took two months of advocating for myself to find the right fit. Because I delivered Kailani out of province, I was provided with all the resources for their service area. I was hopeful that their programs would support me; however,

I didn't qualify because I was from out of province, which I completely understand.

When my care transitioned back to my family physician, he wanted to put a referral in to our local counsellors (none of whom are familiar or specialize in neonatal death). It took two months to finally find a program that was right for me, and I immediately knew that Deb was going to be the perfect fit. How did I know? My intake phone call took an hour, and we discussed what felt like my entire life. At the end of our discussion, she was able to identify the strained relationships I have in my life, why I have gone down certain roads, and how my past experiences were impacting my current relationships. In 2019, I attended a self-discovery seminar with Todd Campbell. During that seminar I came to interpret and figure out why I had selected certain roads in my life and how certain experiences had left such a huge impact and continue to influence my life today. It took thirty years and a three day long intensive seminar to untangle my life and figure this all out, yet she did it in under an hour. Like, *Hello! Yes, do you have room to talk with me daily because I have a lot going on.*

During my intake conversation, she had me completely pegged, and I felt comfortable telling her everything. It was a breath of fresh air. I was able to tell her about all of my previous challenges including experiencing alcoholism with family members, parental divorce, substance misuse, depression, abusive relationships, and eating disorders. I laid all my dirty laundry out to dry, and not once did I feel like she was judging or shaming me.

Therefore, take your time. When you are working with someone, you want it to be a good fit, especially since the topics discussed place us in very vulnerable positions, which can be extremely uncomfortable. You want to find someone who will make you feel as comfortable as possible, which will allow you to truly share what you are thinking and feeling as you move through this challenging time in your life.

COMMUNICATION

O kay, so I did not initially have any intention of talking about communication. However, the more I write and the more topics that come up as I move through this journey of grief, I have started to feel like this is a subject I absolutely need to include. Communication during our grieving period is essential and can make or break so many of our relationships.

Now, communication can be a challenge even when we are not going through significant emotional, physical, and spiritual pain. When we are grieving and experiencing so many emotions at once, communication can become that much more of a task and a challenge. I can say firsthand there are so many times when I have felt like talking was expelling too much of my energy. Not only that, finding the words to relay what I want and express how I am truly feeling has presented as quite a challenging task.

I mean, I've had a long list of family members die; however, the death of my daughter is significantly more impactful in comparison to my previous experiences of grief. Grieving is exhausting. Like holy cheese balls, who knew it was this difficult? I mean, I've grieved the death of my grandparents, aunts, uncles, friends, clients, etc. Death has been everywhere in my life. It was not something new. Yet, Kailani's death was so very different. Something that has helped me significantly this time around has been learning how to communicate effectively, which in turn has aided me in reserving my energy, fostering relationships, and supporting my healing.

Depending on the resource and type of communication you are engaging in, there are different areas you may want to focus on. Because we are focusing on grieving and healing, I will speak more specifically to the areas that have been supportive in helping me within my mourning and grieving journey. There are two models I am going to share with you. The first has three parts and is quite simple as it breaks down into retreat, rethink, and respond.

Retreat

For many of us, we tend to allow our emotions to drive our reactions. I am sure we can all dive into our memory banks and come up with certain situations where something came out of our mouths and we regretted it immediately or shortly after. I am certainly guilty of this, and a couple of these memories continue to make me feel guilty, ashamed, and embarrassed, even though years have passed. I am also certain that 99.9 percent of almost everyone reading this can say that they, too, have done this. And that is okay. *We live* and *we learn* (or that is the goal).

I am going to let everyone in on a bit of a secret. Did you know that when we engage in heated conversations where we become emotionally invested, it triggers our body's fight or flight response? Yes, conversations or even a memory can trigger this response within our bodies. This is why some people start to yell or maybe go quiet when a conversation gets heated; everyone is different. Now, when we are grieving, it makes sense that our emotions are heightened, and we may outwardly express emotions more frequently when interacting with others.

This means that when someone says something like "When you are a mother," or "You can have another child," our body and mind can be triggered, which activates our stress response. Our body physiologically starts going through changes as our heart rate, breathing, and blood flow increase, and certain hormones are released. I admit, when people have said certain things to me like "When you are a mother," I (figuratively) roll up my sleeves and put my fighting mitts on. Part of me goes into my head and starts to think of all the ways I am going to beat the individual to a pulp. If you are someone who can relate, no worries, this is totally natural, and I ask that you please refrain from actually beating anyone.

Truth be told, when we are in this mode, our cognitive capacity—or ability to process information and think clearly—is compromised. In fact, our cognitive capacity drops down to as *low* as thirty percent. What this means is that when we react immediately to what someone is saying when our body's stress response is triggered, our brains are operating at around thirty percent of what they typically do. Hence why we find ourselves in situations where immediately we regret what we say. This is why it is so very important to respond versus react. And we can begin doing this by acknowledging that our emotions are becoming heightened and then pause before we say anything. Therefore, step one is for us to retreat/pause before we respond.

Rethink

Allowing ourselves a moment to think before we respond is something I consider to be a learned skill. First, one must give oneself permission to pause. For many of us, we have developed this discomfort with sitting in silence, and there is this expectation that people want answers, and they want them right now.

By allowing ourselves to step back, take a moment, and simply breathe, we provide the opportunity for our bodies to adjust and process the information we have received. We allow ourselves the opportunity to pause and identify how we are feeling. Angry? Betrayed? Shamed?

This pause also provides us the opportunity to try to gain a new perspective. Is what the person saying to me true? Is the person saying this based on their own values and beliefs? Are my values and beliefs different from theirs?

When we pause, we allow ourselves to re-evaluate and consider different points of view. We can then begin to examine how our responses might affect the outcome of the situation. We can then ask ourselves if there is an opportunity to respond in a way that relays how we think or feel, without creating further conflict, anger, or resentment.

How often do we go back to people in our lives and apologize for something said or done, all because in that moment we were emotionally driven and not thinking rationally? By adopting the retreat, rethink, and respond model, we can begin to cultivate communication methods that encompass a more compassionate, supportive, and engaging approach; one that inspires further communication and discussions instead of anger, resentment, and repression.

Respond

Once we have taken a moment to think about how we are feeling in that moment and look at the situation from different perspectives, we can proceed with *responding* versus *reacting*. Adopting such an approach can allow for meaningful conversations to unfold, especially when they include topics that people do not typically want to discuss, such as PAIL.

Now, in no way, shape, or form am I saying that you must use this three-step technique in your communications. However, I can say from experience that there are times when my responses have been emotionally heated when someone says something that triggers me, and my inner beast is unleashed. It has even resulted in me not having conversations with that person again, or every interaction moving forward is extremely awkward. I usually pride myself on being able to respond versus react, though when it is a discussion about Kailani and how "this is part of the plan," or "you're feeling this way because . . ." I have allowed my emotions to get the best of me. People have no idea what I am thinking or how I am feeling. Although, over time, I have been able to better control my responses and approach these conversations with more understanding and compassion on my part.

The reality is, we are all human and we experience human emotions. Therefore, we are going to say things and do things that we might regret in the minutes, hours, days, weeks, months, or maybe even years that follow. However, acknowledging that we have the ability to control our responses and move away from these occurrences can help decrease or eliminate any regret that may follow. For me, the goal is always about being and doing better in the days that follow, compared to the days that have passed. We cannot change the past, though we can control the now and contribute to a better future.

Awareness Wheel

Another resource I have found helpful in communicating with others when having these difficult conversations is the awareness wheel. Before I dive into this, I want to highlight that the language we use in conversations can make a significant difference in how one receives the information and processes it. For example, when someone says to me, "When you have a baby," I immediately see red, my heart rate goes up, my skin gets hot, my palms begin to sweat, and I am ready to pounce.

However, each time someone says something like this to me, I have come to recognize that I am given the opportunity to react or to respond. For me to respond, I know that I must retreat, rethink, and respond to the individual in non-threatening way.

If I allow myself to simply react, somebody is going to get hurt . . . Alternately, I can use the above retreat, rethink, and respond and apply the awareness wheel, which includes the following aspects:

- *Sensory Data* – this is the information collected through our observations, facts/data, descriptions, or examples.
- *Thoughts* – this includes our own assumptions, beliefs, interpretations, values, or opinions.

- *Feelings* – this includes our emotions toward the topic of conversation, whether this includes frustration, anger, happiness, sorrow, joy, etc.
- *Objectives* – these are our aspirations, hopes, longings, dreams, or goals.
- *Actions* – these are statements of our behaviour, plans, proposals, or activities.

Now, when I use the awareness wheel and think about my *response* to the above comment, it may look something like this:

I carried my child for thirty-one weeks and five days before giving birth to Kailani and holding her in my arms before her heart stopped. I think that my experience of motherhood is very different from others because my baby died. I feel very frustrated when others disregard my experience of motherhood, and I hope that one day people will come to understand that being a parent does not require a child to be living. For those who've had their children die at an older age, they're still considered a parent. Therefore, to help create that awareness, I will continue to share my story of motherhood and the realities of PAIL.

Yes, I am not going to lie, it does take a little bit of thinking, and one must be intentional with their words. However, by using the awareness wheel, I found that I was able to express my own thoughts, feelings, and intentions without placing blame on the person who clearly shares a different set of values and beliefs than I have. This approach has saved me many times, as I have been able to get my message across without coming unglued or beating them over the head. Full disclosure: in my mind, this is exactly what I am doing.

It is important to note that when we use the awareness wheel, we start all our communications off with "I." I feel, I think, I hope, I wish, I desire, I will, etc. This ensures that we make ourselves the focus and not the individual that we are speaking with. If I used "you" in my response, the conversation would look significantly different and might actually result in resentment, regret, and possibly the termination of the relationship, as my response might look something like this:

You do not see me as a mother? You do realize that I carried a baby in me for thirty-one weeks and five days, to then pushed that baby out of my who-ha without any drugs. Your opinions of me and my baby are inaccurate and completely irrelevant. You have no clue what it is like to be in my position of having your baby die in your arms. You have no right to say anything about my situation and are clueless.

Guaranteed, my voice is going to be raised. I will likely have my arms and hands waving around like a raging lunatic, just to make myself appear much bigger and more threatening because you do not dare say anything about me and my baby.

I am quite certain that many of us have been on the receiving end of such an interaction whether it's with strangers, loved ones, or friends. Working in healthcare, I have been on the receiving end of this more times than I can count. I've even been punched in the face. She was a very sweet, very confused, ninety-something-year-old woman. Again, we are human. I do not hold a grudge over individuals who maybe responded in a way that was harvesting anger, hate, resentment, or other malicious feelings. I recognize that I have the ability to control how I show up and act in any situation.

I have come to acknowledge and appreciate that in moments such as these, individuals are experiencing something that I may not fully understand. I also choose not to hold a grudge and practice understanding. I hope that others do the same for me. Though I recognize that when I've been the person who is yelling and screaming at someone else, the individual on the receiving side may not necessarily feel they are in a position to forgive me for my actions. They may even hold a grudge moving forward and, really, that is for them to decide as I cannot control the choices or actions of others. However, I am responsible for my screaming and yelling and can certainly own up to and take responsibility for this.

Every single one of us responds and reacts in different ways to different situations; we do so based on our own values and beliefs that shape our behaviour. Therefore, I want to invite individuals to consider that how we respond and react is completely up to us; each of us has the ability to change the way we think and act in a way that can foster and support not only our communication, but also our relationships.

In the moments where we react, we may find ourselves in the position of saying and doing things that we are not proud of. However, I am happy to report that we do have an opportunity to improve the way we communicate with one another to foster and support our relationships. When we communicate effectively, we can bring awareness to others about our thoughts, feelings, and intentions in a way that is non-judgmental, non-blaming, and non-threatening. We hold the power to our actions.

Again, I offer these as tools as they have assisted me in having some of the most difficult conversations of my life and have allowed me to foster my relationships. We all have the capacity to control our actions and how we respond to these hurtful and unkind situations.

Unfortunately, due to the lack of awareness and knowledge about PAIL, these unkind situations occur more frequently than what would be expected. Now, I am not saying that the responsibility to have these types of conversations lands on grieving parents, because it doesn't. These are tools that everyone can use and apply when having these difficult conversations.

To everyone reading this, I want to highlight that such conversations can present everyone with the opportunity to create safe spaces where we invite individuals to enter into these difficult conversations regarding PAIL and other difficult topics. By doing this, we can work towards increasing awareness, breaking the silence, and join the movement to create changes within our society.

MOURNING, GRIEF, AND SOCIETY

I don't think anyone knows, except for those who live through it, how truly impatient and unkind society can be toward individuals who are grieving pregnancy loss or infant death. I also acknowledge and recognize this expands to losses of all kinds. Death and grief, in general, have a certain stigma and taboo attached to them.

Now, this is not to say that people don't acknowledge an individual's loss and provide support; however, there is a disconnect between acknowledging death versus grief. Grief often isn't acknowledged or accepted, and comments made by others can be extremely hurtful to an individual who is grieving.

For example, comments that suggest that I am not a mother, that I can always have another baby, that my baby is in a "better" place, or any other comment that goes against my own beliefs are extremely hurtful. It is painful when others try to take away or disregard what I am experiencing following the death of my daughter.

The same applies to all individuals who have conceived a child. Regardless of whether an individual has experienced a miscarriage, a stillbirth, or a neonatal death, they are still a parent. They are the parents of the babies who are no longer living, and we all hope to hell that those with living children *never* have to experience the death of their baby or infant. For many of us, we feel it is the most difficult thing one can endure.

So, to everyone out there who thinks that because our children are not living or did not make it to full-term that we are not mothers or fathers, allow me to clarify this misconception. We are mothers. We are fathers. We are parents. However, our experience of parenthood is very different from those with living children. Just because it is different does not give anyone the right to disregard or dismiss the creation and life of our babies, regardless of how short their lives were. If you are someone who has very strong opinions and thoughts about this that are different from the above, it is simple: keep them to yourself. It is okay to have different values and beliefs, though they do not need to be placed on someone who is experiencing PAIL.

Another example I can think of that many individuals have told me: "Forget and move on with your life." Everyone wants to tell you about their sister, aunt, mother, grandmother, and Dorothy from down the road. Because—guess what?—they have all gone through the exact same thing. So get over it.

First off, no one's experience is the same. Furthermore, many individuals who have experienced a miscarriage, stillbirth, or infant death often did not just move on with their life. For many of them, they did not talk about it because it wasn't something accepted or acknowledged by society. So, no, they didn't get over it. They did not forget. They were forced to keep quiet about it and refrain from expressing their grief. Many of them were never given the opportunity to discuss it, feel it, or grieve their loss, and that is truly heartbreaking. And the more we talk about our experiences, the more individuals are coming forward and sharing that they too are one in four.

Just because your aunt or sister or someone in your life has gone through it does not mean that you know the pain they endured or the grief they experienced. People tell me that I don't need to worry because those individuals have all had kids after a miscarriage or neonatal death, and I will too. Therefore, I can just move on with life. Well, guess what? It is just not that simple. Say someone in your life died and I said, "Just get over it. Move on!" How would you feel? Could you just "forget"? Not likely. So, please do not expect me or other grieving parents to simply move on. We can't, and we won't.

Now, I know that in my heart, or at the very least, I choose to believe that these comments are not made to be hurtful or cause pain; quite the opposite, in fact. People often think that by saying this or sharing their own personal stories of losing someone, they are creating a space where they can relate to my experience. However, these comments and stories are not usually helpful. You might have experienced a loved one die, and that was the most challenging and difficult thing you have experienced; however, until you have lived in the other person's shoes, you cannot truly understand because grief is a subjective and individual experience.

By telling me that Dorothy from down the road had babies after her miscarriage or infant loss and that I will too, is not helpful. Providing someone with false hope isn't helpful. There is no guarantee of having a healthy pregnancy or a healthy child down the road. Nothing in life is guaranteed. I know because I am living in this reality with all the other parents who've experienced pregnancy or infant loss.

Not only that, there are so many individuals who've experienced multiple miscarriages, stillbirths, or infant deaths. They've endured multiple losses, and some have not yet had a child survive. Having experienced the death of my daughter, I got to join this horrible club and learn about the *long* list of causes for pregnancy loss and infant death. To be honest, it is rather shocking and mind-blowing that there are so many healthy babies in this world, considering the variety of illnesses and conditions out there.

PAIL rates are one in four. So, on behalf of grieving parents who've lost a child, please refrain from providing false hope and disregarding their current experience of heartbreak and the death of their child. These types of comments imply that a child is replaceable; they are not. When someone's sister, brother, father, mother, grandparent, or anyone dies in someone's life, we don't say to them, "Oh well, at least you have another sister," "You have other friends," or "That is why we are gifted with two sets of grandparents." When in the world did it become okay to say to a grieving parent that they can try for another child?

Furthermore, these types of encounters may result in an individual not wanting to have additional children in the future. From experience, I can say that I have had mixed emotions about this. There are times when I have felt like having a child following Kailani might be an insult to her memory or reduce my memory of her. In hindsight, I truly believe that the only reason I have felt this way is because society perpetuates the belief that by having another baby, we are replacing the one we lost. This is not true.

I know that having a baby in the future will not replace or reduce Kailani's memory. But these thoughts were part of my grieving process. It took time to work through these thoughts and emotions. To move through them, I needed to utilize a variety of resources and supports to transition away from this way of thinking. Regardless, there are many individuals who have experienced a significant amount of trauma due to their pregnancy or infant loss, which has resulted in them not wanting to risk it again in the future. That long list I mentioned previously and not having a guarantee in life is definitely overwhelming. The thought of possibly going through this again is terrifying. Therefore, do not assume that the person is ready or wanting to move forward with future pregnancies.

Now, before I dive into this next section, I want to clarify the terms I use. I will use the term "griever" to represent the individual grieving the death of a loved one or other loss. And for those who are offering the griever support, I use the term "supporters." This is not to say that the supporter is not also grieving their own losses; however, they are taking a supportive role in that moment.

This next section is a means to help individuals better understand ways in which they might be able to provide support to anyone who is grieving. This is for both those in supportive positions and those who are grieving. On a side note, I have found that individuals who have also experienced a significant loss in their life are a little more familiar with how to best support someone experiencing grief. The reality is that sometimes the best way to learn and understand how to support someone through loss is through the experience itself.

Reactions to Grief

People around you may not always know what to say or how to support you. I've found many individuals would say or message me things like, "There are no words," or "I don't know what to say." Honestly, I became grateful for these responses, as this was much preferred over things like, "Time heals all wounds," and the other comments I've listed previously.

You may even find that individuals with whom you were close, prior to the death of a loved one, are now distancing themselves. I had a handful of people in my life reach out weeks after Kailani's birth and death to apologize for not being in contact and to tell me they just didn't know what to say. There are individuals whom I was close with prior to Kailani's birth and death that I have not heard from, even seven months following. Note to supporters: this approach of distancing can be hurtful and sometimes misinterpreted by the griever. When people distance themselves, it's not always seen as a way to give people "space," although there is an internal dialogue that the griever may be having, and that inner voice is telling a very different story.

I appreciate how these experiences can also impact the supporter; however, taking a moment to say, "I am here for you if you need me," or "I am thinking of you today" truly makes all the difference in the world. Just knowing that there are individuals who are there for you during such a challenging time provides a sense of reassurance. So for those that don't know what to do, do the smallest thing. Tell the person you're thinking of them or that you are there for them. You do not need to have all the answers or shy away from the griever for weeks or months to try and figure out what to say; keep it simple.

There are times when the griever and/or supporter may change how they interact with those around them. It is important for us to discuss this as I recognize that for many, people take this personally, and it can have a significant impact on relationships. To help support relationships during times of grief, it is important to explore why individuals may select to distance themselves from others and take time to understand where each person is coming from.

Distancing by the Supporter

Now, I have discovered that this works both ways. Isolation and distancing can occur by both parties; the griever and the supporter. It is important to acknowledge and respect one's wishes in both cases. Though, I might suggest that this behaviour of isolation be used carefully as it may cause more hurt and heartache, versus what one might experience having not gone down this road. Some reasons that individuals might select to distance themselves from the griever may include:

- They might not know what to say to you and feel that they need to "fix it," resulting in them distancing from the griever as they don't know how to help them.
- If the supporter went through a similar experience, this may bring about and resurface their grief from their loss.
- In some cases, the "supporter" may also be the "griever." An example of this might be a husband/wife who has lost a child. This can be complicated as there may be different expectations from the parties involved.

These are just a few examples. However, know this: distancing oneself away from someone, especially without the other knowing and understanding why, can be very hurtful. How does one overcome these challenges, you might ask? Well, it is not necessarily without difficulty. Yet there are a couple of approaches one might wish to take.

First, and most important, as the supporter, you are not responsible for "fixing it." Simply offer your support and be there for your loved one or friend by offering a listening ear and ensuring they know that you're there for them. This is why I use the term "supporter" and not "fixer."

I might suggest avoiding questions like "Are you okay?" or "How can I fix it?" The reality is you can't fix it and no, we are not okay. Read that again and allow it to sink in. I am sorry that I am the one to tell you this, though it is the reality. The only way to fix this situation is for our babies to be alive again. I know that many individuals want to make the situation better, though there are times when we cannot, and this is one of those times.

Second, in cases where the griever's situation is a reminder of your own loss, first acknowledge that it is a trigger of your own grief. Whether or not you feel like you're in a place to support the griever in what they are experiencing, acknowledge where you are at and honour your grief. If you do not feel that you can be a support at this time, that is okay.

I might suggest relaying how you are feeling and be open to having that conversation about how your own grief has been triggered. This may provide a means for both parties to acknowledge and understand the realities each person is facing. I strongly advise against ghosting the griever or avoiding them, as this may cause more pain and harm to the relationship.

Consider being open to communicating and maybe even using the communication tools discussed previously. This may allow the opportunity to relay and express how each party is feeling in a way that supports and fosters the relationship moving forward. In my opinion, honesty is the best policy.

If you feel like you could be a support person, although you are struggling because their situation is triggering your own grief, consider exploring this more. Maybe this is an opportunity to connect with the griever on a deeper level. One of my friends had lost her husband years ago and because of her experience with grief and loss, it allowed us to connect on a deeper level. Not only that, it was a great opportunity for her to share the many positive memories she had of her husband and how life has been since. By focusing on those positive memories, she has been able to move forward in her grief.

Sometimes, your experience of grief may contribute to the way the griever is able to connect with you. Your lived experience may even be an opportunity to help others in navigating through their grief.

Distancing by the Griever

Now, in many cases, grievers may experience an overwhelming number of individuals lending their support and reaching out to say they are there for you. However, the griever may not be prepared to connect with individuals and may choose to distance or isolate themselves for various reasons:

- When someone dies unexpectedly, the griever(s) may not have had an opportunity to prepare themselves for life without the individual who has passed. This can be very overwhelming and result in an individual pulling away from people as they try to grapple with what is now their new reality.
- Supporters/grievers might remind the griever of the deceased. For example, my best friend was pregnant at the same time I was, which was a bit of a trigger for me.
- Grievers may isolate and distance themselves because they feel like a "downer." Grieving can be very emotional and, to be honest, I frequently feel like the buzz kill. It feels like people around us are often cautious about what they say; sometimes people start crying when they see someone who is grieving; over time, people seem to get frustrated that grievers are not back to their "old" self, etc.

Again, this is not an extensive list and there are many other reasons why someone might isolate; these are just some of the reasons I isolated for a time. For supporters, please know that it is nothing personal, and please continue to keep an eye on your friend or loved one. If you notice that someone is distancing or isolating themselves to a point that could be detrimental to the griever's health and wellness, be sure to seek support as appropriate.

I recall someone in my life whom I didn't see for over a year; I imagine that she took that time to figure out how to be in this life without her significant other. And guess what? This was okay because she had supports in place.

The challenge comes when an individual is isolating themselves to a point where they won't let anyone in, especially over time. When Matt and I were in the hospital, our families kept asking if we wanted them there with us. They had flights lined up, bags packed, and vehicles loaded for when we told them yes. However, we both felt that it would be too challenging to have them there, and we needed to go through this on our own and figure it out.

We felt like having them present would just be so much harder (I would have been counselling my mom and she knows it). Then, when we got home, I didn't want to see anyone. My mom asked if I wanted her there, and I knew that me saying no broke her heart. However, she respected my wishes. She dropped Gibson off at our house before we arrived and then went home.

Of course, I knew it was killing my mom not to see us, so I asked her to come the next day. Then, in the weeks following, we slowly began to open up our circle again. To be honest, I didn't want to. However, I knew that I needed to. I found it easiest to connect with others who had experienced a significant loss in their life because they could relate to grief, and it made me feel less alone in this journey.

Through these types of experiences, it is important to have support in our lives and leverage them. Individuals may choose to utilize support outside their immediate circle of family and friends, which is great. Regardless, it is essential that as a griever, we use whatever means of support that aids us in our healing journey in a non-destructive and healthy way.

It is when someone pushes everyone out of their life and then starts going down this dark spiralling path that we need to become concerned. Watch for this, as depression is a very real concern and has a long list of complications. For a period, I struggled with this and really was not sure if I was going down a road to depression. Fortunately, I was able to talk it out with my counsellor. With her help, I was able to identify what behaviours would cause the alarm bells to ring to indicate that it was not just grief that I was experiencing, but also depression.

For individuals who have given birth and had their baby die, it is important to note that postpartum depression is still a concern and a risk. I am not going to go into the signs/symptoms, though I will suggest that you might want to talk to your doctor about this. If you're concerned about someone in your life going down this road, become familiar with the signs/symptoms and what you can do to provide support. Postpartum depression and depression are very real concerns that can have significant consequences. It is important that these behaviours be noted and followed up on appropriately.

Note, the griever may not want help from others and may refuse it. It isn't easy watching someone spiral into darkness; however, we cannot force ourselves on individuals. When I look back in my life during times when I was severely depressed, I am grateful that there were people who cared about me and offered their support. I didn't seek their support during that time, though that experience provided me with some life lessons for the future. Thanks to them, I knew that I did not need to go through anything alone and there were people watching over me to ensure I didn't inflict any type of self-harm.

If you are someone who might be at this point, know you are not alone. I found it easiest to go through this process by taking each day step by step, minute by minute. Life moving forward is not going to be the same, and it takes time to process and transition into this new life and this new you. I say this "new" you because grieving the death of someone significant in our lives does not leave us the same. It does have a significant impact and can change who we are and how we see the world moving forward. So, take the time to discover this new you. Allow yourself to not feel okay, but recognize that you do not need to do this alone and through the darkness, believe that there will be light again. Also, if you are experiencing suicidal ideations or have been inflicting self-harm, please reach out to a care provider and seek support. You matter and are loved.

How to Support a Grieving Individual

Grief can be life changing. Though, grief doesn't have to be life changing in an all-consuming, negative way. Grief can change life in the most beautiful way, and conversations about grief can bring people closer together. So why is it that as a society in North America, there seems to be a negative stigma that encompasses death and grief? Maybe if we start talking about our experiences more, we can help change the narrative and change these predetermined views.

As a supporter, when you reach out to the griever, don't take offence if the individual does not connect or provide you with a response. You may even want to acknowledge in your communications that there is no expectation that the griever contacts you. Grieving is very complex and talking about their experience is often not something that people want to engage in immediately following their loss.

Talking about the experience can be very challenging for the griever, and sometimes people need a minute to truly feel and absorb what it is they've just gone through. I didn't fully grasp everything until I was into my second week. Therefore, please acknowledge and respect that the griever may not be in a place to communicate with others and may want to spend time on their own. When they are ready, they may choose to reach out. What is important is ensuring that the griever knows that you are there for them as a supporter.

Something I would like to highlight for individuals, I have found that many individuals that are going through the grieving process have experienced negative feedback when talking to another about their loss. This can impact whether or not an individual will talk with others about it in the future. For this reason, I strongly encourage the application of specific listening techniques. When individuals provide responses that are triggering or hurtful, some people may opt to stop talking about their experience, which can result in an interruption of the grieving process and may be detrimental to their healing.

Therefore, to all the supporters out there, when an individual comes to you to share their story, it is simple. There is really only one thing individuals need to do: listen. This is required regardless of how much time has passed since the person's loss. (I will touch on this shortly.) And I mean truly *listening*. Did you know there are different levels of listening that we practice? I have included a brief description of the three levels here for reference:

1. During this interaction, the listener's primary focus is internal. The listener is focused on their own thoughts, feelings, opinions, and judgments. The individual takes what they hear and focuses on how it relates to them and their own experiences. When this occurs, the listener's responses change the focus from the griever to the supporter. Many individuals feel that by using an experience of their own, they can relate to the griever. However, I want to remind you that all experiences are subjective. Your experience may not be received as truly relatable and may be taken as though you, the listener, are devaluing the griever's experience.

2. When an individual uses level two listening approaches, they focus on the griever's words, sounds, and expressed emotions through the body language, facial expression(s), and tone of voice the griever is using. The listener may use approaches like paraphrasing and repeating things back to the individual. By doing this, the listener is able to demonstrate their understanding.

3. The last level and deepest level of listening takes skill and requires individuals to follow their intuition. This is a form of communication used by coaches to really engage an individual in conversations. When this type of listening is applied, level two listening approaches are used in addition to the use of the listener's intuition. For example, have you ever felt like someone

had more to say, but was holding back for some reason? When using this level of listening, you might ask a question to encourage the individual to share more as you are picking up that there is more to the story than what is being said.

Through the use of level two listening, individuals can ensure that others feel heard and valued. This can be very transformational as many individuals go through life feeling undervalued and not heard in many aspects of their life. This may have something to do with the fact that many of us were brought up believing that kids are seen and not heard. Unfortunately, for many of us, this has resulted in this belief following us through into adulthood. It took me a long time to find my voice because of this belief. However, as supporters, we can help individuals find their voice, and the best way to do this is through listening. Therefore, be open and available to simply listen and expand your listening skills. This is one of the best ways to support someone who is grieving the death of a loved one.

Sympathy Gifts

A common tradition that is practised by many individuals in various regions, cultures, and religions is that of sympathy gifts. A sympathy gift is sent from supporters to grievers, or to the funeral home, as an expression of condolence. To be honest, I am all for doing whatever supporters feel best to show their love and support to someone who is grieving. Whether it is through making meals, sending flowers, gift certificates, postcards, formal bereavement gifts, etc., do what feels right to you. The thought behind these actions and the intention behind them is sincerely appreciated.

Now, for me and Matt, neither of us wanted to come home to a house full of sympathy flowers and meals. For me, they would have been a reminder, and I didn't want everything around me to be a reminder of what we had just experienced. I mean, I had the nursery and the baby items at home that I was already concerned about. I didn't want condolence gifts everywhere. Furthermore, if I had a bunch of meals prepared and made for me, I know I would have struggled to move back into a structured routine. So, we did something a little different.

Matt and I decided that the best way for our friends, family, and acquaintances to show their love and support was by donating back to the hospital that helped us through such a traumatic experience. To do this, we simply asked individuals wanting to show their love and support through gifts to provide a donation to the hospital unit in Kailani's name.

As others will, unfortunately, experience similar situations, we felt that if we could encourage others to support the medical system, this might help improve and increase their resources and help the system to better help others. For us, this approach felt most meaningful and brought a sense of purpose to the experience of losing our daughter. We felt that instead of money being spent on expensive bouquets of flowers that would die, the money donated would be used in an effective and beneficial way that might prevent others from going through what we had experienced.

To the individual who is grieving, do what you feel is best in supporting you and what you need in your grieving process. Be direct with those around you if there is something you prefer as a means to support you and/or your family or honour your loved one. We do not have to follow the "rules" that have been set and are allowed to take a different approach. And as supporters, honour and respect the wishes of the grieving individual(s) if they do request that others take a new approach to showing or expressing their love and support.

Eliminate Expectations and Timeframes

There is no timeline or end period to grief. Please go back and read that again.

One of the most common comments made toward grievers is this, "It's been (insert number of months/years)," followed by something like, "It is time to move on," or "You should be over it by now." I find this often comes from individuals that have never truly experience grief.

For those with no previous experience of grief, it is simple: do not pretend to know what the person is going through or direct them in what to do. By saying that you know how they are feeling, you are only making matters worse and the person is likely envisioning strangling you or hitting you over the head. Not even kidding; this comes up in almost all group discussions that I have participated in.

What you can do, though, is say something like, "I cannot imagine what you are experiencing right now," because honesty is the best policy. Keep in mind, this statement is not accepted by everyone, though. Therefore, it might be best to say something like, "if you would like a listening ear, I am here for you," or "you are in my thoughts and I am sending you love."

Honestly, if you do not understand why someone is grieving the way they are and for the length of time that they are, be grateful that you do not know their pain. Because it friggin' sucks. When someone close to you dies, you become part of the grief group. There are also subgroups to these. For example, individuals who experience a miscarriage or infant loss do not just join the grief group—they also join the PAIL group. Trust us when we say it is not something you want to ever know or experience, though this little exercise might help individuals better understand.

If you have not yet had someone you are extremely close to die, I want you to think about this for a minute. I want you to think about who you are closest with in your life. This might be a family member or a friend; it does not matter. Whoever it is you choose, I want it to be the person you feel most connected to in this lifetime. Got them in your mind?

Now, imagine how it might feel if you were to lose them all of a sudden. How drastically your life would change. How you would no longer be able to go to them for all the things you did before. How the person you felt most connected to in this world and who might have known you the best is no longer here with you. The person you have made so many plans with and was part of every aspect of your life is now gone. Now, tell me . . . when should I expect you to get over it and no longer have thoughts and feelings toward that person? Can you honestly give me a timeline?

Some of you may feel that this is a mean exercise and, honestly, it is meant to get a point across. I highly doubt that anyone can give me an actual timeframe because the thoughts, feelings, and memories you have of that loved one don't just disappear. To be honest, the only way you can eliminate them is if you were to forget the person altogether. Is that something anyone really wants? Because along with the pain and heartbreak of their death, all the good memories go as well. How much of your life and memories would be erased?

So, on behalf of grievers, I ask that individuals eliminate any expectations held toward grievers that we should be "over it" and "move forward" with life because a certain amount of time has passed. It is not realistic.

I also ask that grievers eliminate any expectations you may have placed on yourselves to get over your grief. You are not expected to move on because a specific amount of time has passed. We all have the choice to move forward in life when we are ready and on our own time. Honour and acknowledge whatever amount of time it takes and know there is no "getting over it," although there is an opportunity to move forward with your grief.

Language

Let us take a moment to talk about language. When interacting with individuals experiencing grief, language can be key in how one might feel best supported and connected to you. For example, some individuals do not like when others use alternate phrases or terms to refer to death such as "loss," "moved on," "went home," "passed," etc.

The easiest way to determine what kind of language to use with a person is through listening. If someone says, "My daughter has died," or "My husband is with the angels now," take this as an opportunity to connect through language. Mirror the language that the griever uses.

By listening and mimicking the language that the griever uses, individuals can avoid comments that may agitate or anger the individual. For example, people have said to me, "Kailani is in a better place now" and "It's all part of God's plan," though this is not my belief. While this is their belief, I do not share this opinion. The only place Kailani should be is in my arms—plain and simple. Individuals who know me well know that my beliefs do not align with the idea of a Heaven or God taking care of my child. Yes, I do call Kailani my angel and believe she is with me, though my beliefs of a higher power and life after death are very different than what others believe.

Over time, I have been able to adopt the appropriate communication methods and tools I need to respond, though this example highlights why it is crucial to understand the thoughts, feelings, and beliefs of the griever through listening and meeting them where they are.

Laughter During Loss

Now, if you know someone really well, trust your instincts. Receiving the news that Kailani was not compatible with our world was devastating. Having her die shortly after birth was soul crushing. However, Matt and I still took the opportunity to laugh and joke around about life leading up to her birth. Those who are in the medical professions know that we tend to use humour frequently during these dark times. Why? Because if life just piled up with sadness, anger, and resentment, we would all be miserable, all the time; and who wants that? Personally, I use humour as a means to cope, as everyone has likely gathered, based on my writing. I've been this way for as long as I can remember, and I acknowledge it.

I remember as a teenager in high school, one of my close friends experienced a miscarriage. I was the one who drove her to the hospital and sat at the bedside with her in the emergency room. When I think back on this now, I feel like the joke I made was not my finest moment; yet, together, we laughed. And even years after that experience, she told me that she was grateful that I was there and that I helped her during that time because I was able to make her laugh. So, trust your instincts.

Interactions and conversations following the death of a loved one can cause some anxiety, and that is totally natural. Sometimes laughter is needed during such challenging times, though I would not recommend joking about the loss or the experience. However, joking around can sometimes lighten the mood, and a dose of laughter may be needed. Use your judgment. Again, you know your friend/family member best.

Remember, part of the healing and grieving process is to allow joy and sadness to be present together throughout all experiences of life. So, it may not be humour you use, though instead you may choose to share a favorite memory of the individual as a means to remember and honour them and who they were. This can definitely be more challenging when it involves PAIL, so be sure to use these approaches as deemed appropriate. For example, Kailani had tons of hair when she was born, and she was early at thirty-one weeks and six days. Her hair was so long, you could see the curls she got from her daddy. Joking around about how long her hair would have been, should we have made it to full term, would have put a smile on my face. I love talking about my daughter and all aspects of her.

Talk About Grief

Be open to talking about grief to support the normalization of this experience. If you have gone through the death of someone and grieved them, this is a way to relate to the griever; not in the way that you know what they are feeling, but as a means to understand that grief is complex. Avoid saying things like you know how they are feeling and know what they are going through. Instead, ask how they are managing in their grief or ask about their experience. If the griever tells you that all they do is cry, support them in that experience. Avoid telling people that they *need* to "stop crying," or "be grateful for what they have." This is their individual experience, so support them in however they are feeling and expressing those emotions (so long as they are not bringing harm to their self or others).

If you have experienced grief before, you likely remember how you felt or continue to feel as part of the journey. If you have found a method that helped you in your own grief, depending on your relationship with the individual, you may choose to share that. Though, again, I might suggest avoiding saying things like "you should," or "you will," or "it will" statements.

The griever does not need to follow instructions, nor do they necessarily want to use the methods you recommend. Just because "I wrote a book and it helped" does not mean that someone else should do the same. It is not guaranteed to help them, though I am happy to share the methods I have implemented that have supported me in this journey, which is why I wrote about it. Though my messaging continues to be this: take what resonates and leave what does not.

So, if you have a method that worked for you, approach this in a supportive and sensitive way. Ensure to always recognize and acknowledge that their experience is completely their own and everyone's grief journey is different. Focus on how they are feeling and try to support them through that.

An example I have is what my co-worker and friend did for me. She gifted me a rose bush to create a memorial space, if I so choose. She made it clear that this gesture was not to pressure me into it or anything, although it was something that she found helpful in navigating through the grief she experienced after her husband died and she wanted to present me with this as an option.

She was also able to incorporate some humour into the situation, as before she presented it to me, she said, "You are probably going to kill me for this." She knew that I have struggled my whole life with having a brown thumb and have not had a good history of keeping plants alive. In this moment, she made me laugh while also providing a new method and option for me to honour my baby girl, which I truly appreciated. (Update status on the rose bush: sadly, it didn't make it through the winter though I am continuing to build my gardening skills).

Say Their Name

When people die, it's as if individuals become scared to say the person's name; and I do recognize that in some cultures it is considered taboo. However, this doesn't need to be a one size fits all approach. Not saying the person's name contributes to the stigma around death. Also, by not saying the person's name, you are not lessening the grief and heartache of grieving individuals; it actually makes it worse. Additionally, by avoiding the use of someone's name, it can contribute to delayed healing for the griever. There is no changing the reality that those we love have died. Though it doesn't mean that they didn't exist.

Now, through my experience and many conversations with others who've experienced the death of a loved one, I know that many individuals get frustrated by this. The majority of parents' love hearing the name of their child. Yes, it brings up memories and feelings. However, just because someone avoids using a child or individual's name does not mean that those memories and feelings disappear or do not exist. In fact, people avoiding the use of our child's name creates more anguish and heartache. Therefore, say their name. We think about them daily, and they are part of our family. So, say their name.

From my own experience, I can honestly say that this behaviour has actually made it uncomfortable for me to even talk about my grief at times. With some individuals, I've even shied away from telling them my daughter's name, which is absolutely ridiculous! I should not be concerned about how someone else is going to react to hearing my daughter's name. I love her name and I want to shout it from the rooftops: KAILANI! I love hearing her name; it is so beautiful and I love every memory I have of her, even though there are not many. So please, say their names. These are our children, our loved ones, and we speak their names.

Save the Date(s)

Depending on who the person was or their relationship to the griever, there may be specific dates of importance; for example, birthdays, anniversaries, holidays, due dates, etc. If you are familiar with these dates, I might suggest taking note of them.

September 20, 2020, was my due date for Kailani. I woke up that morning and the tears would not stop. That was the day I had been preparing for throughout my entire pregnancy. It was a difficult day. I also received loving messages and phone calls from a couple of family members and honestly, it warmed my heart that they remembered and reached out to me. They took the time to check in and knew that it might be a difficult day for me. Having that ongoing support makes a world of a difference.

Therefore, save the date(s). Reach out to the individual and acknowledge that it was a significant day and that you want to check in with them. Maybe the griever has some type of way they celebrate or mourn the individual on these days. Be a willing participant and support them in these traditions. Just be there, no matter what length of time passes, because there will always be the milestones, the anniversary dates, and the holidays that trigger the what-ifs and should-have-been moments in our lives.

Dos and Don'ts

Now, there are a couple of items that can make or break a relationship when it comes to supporting someone through loss and grief. Here is a breakdown of the dos and don'ts. I've also included a list of what people would like individuals to say and what to avoid. These are listed under the "say this" and "avoid saying" lists.

Individuals may be shocked to see some things listed under the "not this" list; however, each of these comments has been made by others toward grieving mothers or fathers. This list is not extensive by any stretch of the imagination, but these are common comments that people have received.

Dos	Do NOT's
• Offer support through listening • Use level two or three listening skills • Follow your instincts and intuition on how to support your loved one • Use and mimic the language that the griever is using • Acknowledge and support the person in whatever feelings they are feeling (there is no right or wrong) • Remember important dates (anniversaries, birthdays, etc.) • Honour the deceased with the griever in whichever way they choose	• Use level one listening • Provide fake promises and false hope • Use language that disregards the griever's experience or goes against their values and beliefs • Take it personally • Pretend to know what the person is feeling and experiencing • Expect a person to be the same following the death of a loved one • Advise the person how to manage their grief • Avoid using the deceased's name • Avoid the griever • Avoid conversations about the deceased • Place or force your beliefs on the griever

Say this	Avoid Saying
• I am here to support you. • If you ever need someone to listen, I am here. • The deceased's name, if they have one. • It is okay to not be okay. • It wasn't your fault. • You are not alone. • Is there anything I can do to support or help you? • Offer specific support without asking. Examples might include household tasks like mowing the lawn, offering to take the kids for a play date on a specific day, etc. Anything that might help the griever a bit.	• Are you okay? • At least you have other kids. • You can always have another child. • When are you going to try again? • It is time to get over it. • Stop living in the past. • Look at it as a blessing. • Just give your body a rest. • You don't need any more kids. • It is God's plan. • This was God's way of saying your son/daughter wasn't going to be perfect. • You brought it on yourself. • It just wasn't meant to be. • You're a bad mother. You're incapable of being a mother. • He/she is in a better place. • Think about your other children. • Good thing it happened early and not at birth. • Others have had it worse than you. • You'll be a mom, one day. • You weren't far along, so it wasn't a baby yet. • If you make it to twenty-four weeks, your baby has a better chance to survive. • It wasn't your time to be a mommy. • That you know about other people who've gone through the exact same thing and they have babies now, so they too will have babies in the future. • Ask about the cause of death or miscarriage. Example: "Did you lift something heavy to cause your miscarriage?" • Blame the mother for the child's death or question motives. • Anything that begins with "at least…" ex. At least you know you can get pregnant.

Notice how the "say this" list is significantly shorter than the list under "avoid saying". This is for a reason. The supporter should be in the position of listening, meaning that they should allow the griever to speak eighty percent of the time. As a supporter, you are not required to say much of anything; therefore, do not feel obligated to do so.What is best is that you provide a listening ear and truly hear what the grieving individual is saying. Allow them to talk about it and support them in whatever they are feeling, for however long they are feeling it. This truly is the best way to help an individual who is experiencing grief.

Ring Theory

Now, my counsellor shared an article with me that explains what is known as "ring theory." I want to share this with individuals, as it provides a good baseline and guide on how not to say the wrong thing to a grieving individual. To be honest, this can be applied to all types of crises and is not limited to mourning and grief. For simplicity, I will demonstrate using my own personal relationships.

To begin, I draw a circle. Being the individual who has experienced Kailani's death in the most intimate and direct way, I represent the centre of the ring. Figure 1 provides a brief overview of how one would proceed to create their own ring theory. Once you have completed the diagram, it is referred to as having a Kvetching order.

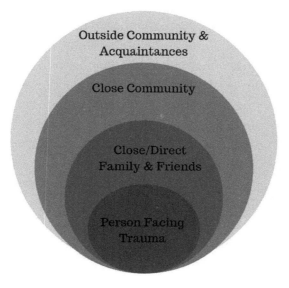

Figure 1: Ring Theory of Kvetching. Comfort in, dump out.

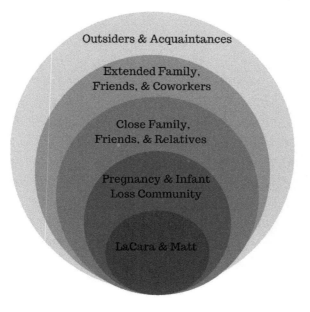

Figure 2: LaCara's Kvetching Order

The way that this works is simple. The closer an individual is to the trauma or loss, the more individuals they are able to "dump" out to. When an individual is speaking with someone in a smaller ring than them, the goal is to simply help. The goal is to provide comfort and support. This means that if the person you are speaking with is closer to the trauma, you do not get to express your own frustrations or give advice. You simply provide the person with comfort and support.

I know, I know. But who do you get to dump on if the person you are talking with is in a smaller circle? Well, you get to dump onto anyone who is in a bigger circle than yourself. You can share how shocked you are, cry, feel absolutely horrible, and express your frustrations in an outward fashion to those in larger circles. However, when you are speaking to someone inward toward the small circle, the only thing that gets to go in is comfort and support.

There is absolutely nothing wrong with individuals feeling and saying specific things toward a given situation. Though one must be cautious of who one is saying it to, especially when it is not you that is in the centre of the ring. As much as we all want to provide advice, share our values, beliefs, and wisdom, this is not a mutual feeling. Often, people develop anger and resentment toward individuals who say the wrong thing. And just know that the wrong thing can change from one person to the next.

If you are not in the middle of the ring, take a moment to evaluate where you might be located. Take a moment to evaluate where the person you are speaking with might be located. And from there, determine what might be appropriate or inappropriate to say and share. For those who are feeling frustrated with this approach, just know this: you might not be in the centre of the circle right now, though your time will come. When it does, you can express yourself in whatever way you need to, to whomever you would like. As they say, sharing is caring, and we will all get our turn.

Communication with Supporters

Now, I acknowledge that when going through the grieving process, it can be a challenge to reach out and talk to others about what one is experiencing. I get it. To be completely honest, I really did not feel like reaching out to individuals for the first couple of months. I mean, I had no interest in talking to anyone and definitely had no interest in seeing people. However, I might suggest that grievers provide feedback to their supporters, even if it is a small message to relay their appreciation and gratitude if someone has reached out.

I found that the number of messages I received to be quite overwhelming. Now, just in case the future has some new way of communicating, I say "messages" because back in this day and age, individuals reached out via social media, text message, or through a gift. Most of my responses back to messages were a simple "Thank you," or I had someone relay my gratitude back to family and friends for me.

For my coworkers, I wrote up an email and asked a friend and co-worker to send it to everyone. That allowed me an opportunity to thank them for their love, support, and the goodies they sent without having to try to get everyone's emails or receive a bunch of replies. I truly appreciate every single one of them, and it warms my heart, knowing that I am in their thoughts.

Here is the thing: I know that during times of grief, we sometimes feel like we want to shut everyone out. However, I ask individuals to place themselves in their supporters' shoes—this provides a different perspective. If one of my friends, family, or coworkers were going through something like this, I would want to know that they were okay. I would worry if they ghosted me, especially if I previously had a close relationship or connection to them. People do appreciate knowing that you are okay, even if it doesn't come directly from you. Therefore, I encourage individuals to have some method of letting people know you are okay—or not okay, though alive.

I do believe that expressing our appreciation and gratitude toward our supporters further inspires individuals to want to continue to support us. It is kind of like the saying "if you say no too often, people will stop asking." If people keep offering their support and only ever get ghosted and don't hear anything back, eventually that support may no longer be available. Therefore, I do invite individuals to take the time to say "thank you" in whatever way feels best.

Personally, throughout my experience I continued to provide updates in my Facebook group. It allowed me an opportunity to thank everyone for their love and support while also giving them little updates on where I was at in my grieving journey. For me, this eliminated the need to have the same conversation over and over again. It also allowed people to see my face when I chose to do video updates, which I know many people were grateful for—especially since the COVID-19 pandemic had isolated us from one another in the months leading up to this whole experience.

This approach is definitely not for everyone. Though, I know that more and more people are starting to leverage technology in various ways to share their stories and connect with others.

Now, to close this chapter, I would like to leave grieving mothers and fathers with this. The death of your child will never get easier; however, there is opportunity to move forward with your grief and welcome happiness into this new life. There will always be that void and yearning in your heart, but in our grief, we have the option to allow joy and happiness to be present in our lives. I do believe that our little ones want us to live a happy and healthy life, even in their absence.

Someone in a PAIL support group I was part of shared a poem. It has brought comfort to many individuals, including myself. So, I would like to share it with you.

AN ANGEL'S STORY

There once was a procession of children marching in heaven.

Each child held a lighted candle, and as they marched, they sang.

Their faces shone with happiness. But one little girl stood alone.

"Why don't you join us, little girl?" one happy child asked.

"I can't," she said. "Every time I light my candle
my mother puts it out with her tears."

Author Unknown

PERMISSION TO HEAL

I've worked as a wound care nurse, and I can honestly tell you some bad things can happen when a person does not care for their wounds. I have had clients who have neglected self-care, which resulted in their wound becoming infected. I have even had clients who had to have limbs amputated and, in some cases, we could not stop the infection, leading to death. I mean, there were many things that occurred in between, though my point is that time alone does not heal. For a wound to become a scar, there are certain factors that come into play, and we must create a supportive environment for healing, which includes directly caring for the wound and also changing other aspects of our lifestyle.

Something that I learned throughout this process is that in order to start healing, I had a choice to make. I needed to intentionally give myself permission to heal. People say that time heals wounds, though the reality is that if we do not take the time to care for those wounds, they will not heal. Not only that, even after they've healed, we carry a scar that remains with us forever. Time alone does not heal, and healing does not mean to fix. Therefore, when I use the terms *heal* or *healing*, I specifically mean mechanisms and methods that help lift or lighten the weight that resulted from Kailani's death.

If we do not give ourselves permission to heal, the focus can remain on the negative aspects of our experiences: what we've lost; how life will never be the same; how life, without our loved one, has no meaning or purpose. Doing this can delay and impact our ability to heal. More so, we create this ongoing weight that can be all-suffocating and impossible to carry. We deserve so much more in life, and the first step is to give ourselves permission to take steps in helping to lift that weight.

I ask you, are you ready to embark on this journey? Do you want to move forward? If yes, I invite you to embrace both grief and joy in your life. Because part of the healing journey through grief requires us to allow both sorrow and happiness to be present.

Through my communications and interactions with others in the grieving process, many have never truly felt like they have been given the opportunity to heal. This has been related to mindset, societal views and impacts, and the type of support system they had access to during their journey. There are so many different factors that contribute to and impact our ability to manage our grief. Reality check, though: it is in our power to figure things out and find what works for us. Grief is personal. It is a unique and individualized journey. There is no one size fits all approach. Therefore, are you willing to explore what works best for you? Yes, I admit that it is work. Grief is a challenge and discovering new ways to help carry this moving forward takes time and effort.

However, as you move through this, I invite you to remember that there is no one way to do grief or move forward in your healing journey. Grief does not allow us to "get to the other side." We must approach grief and the internal dialogue we use within ourselves in a very specific and intentional way. By doing this, we can ensure it does not block or delay us in our grieving and healing journeys. Therefore, take a moment to observe yourself and the language you use.

Time and time again I had had people tell me that they *cannot* and will never be the same, which is true. However, for some, living becomes a burden in the sense that they see their life having also come to an end. There are times when the death of a loved one is translated into being unable to do A, B, or C, because their loved one is no longer living, and they aren't either. When the people we love die, this does not mean that we die with them. Yes, a piece of me died with Kailani. However, I am still here, very much alive and breathing (even though some days I would prefer to be with my daughter). Although a piece of me died with her, a new piece of me was born—a very broken and shattered piece. By doing nothing and by not being an active participant in my life, I am making the choice to live in misery and sadness. I don't want this reality, and I believe that Kailani would not want this for me either.

When I went to a grief education session shortly after Kailani's death, one of the women present said that she and her husband had all these plans to travel the world. However, because he died, she can't do anything without him and so remains at home—alone. In some cases, people become "stuck" in the transition to life after the death of a loved one, and that is okay. However, the weight of this can be exhausting. Based on my observations of her and the language she used, the weight of losing her husband was becoming heavier instead of lighter.

As the discussion moved forward, it was evident that this individual had no intention of moving forward in her grief. However, I share this story because I invite you to observe yourself. Are you living in a mindset of scarcity, where the death of your loved one—whether it is a child, husband, wife, partner, friend, etc.—is all-encompassing and crippling, where you feel you cannot go on? Or is there an opportunity to look at this experience differently and give yourself permission to move forward with this grief?

Matt and I took a different approach. Because we opted to have Kailani cremated, we felt that having jewellery made with her ashes allowed her to be with us always. Therefore, when we travel to new and exciting places, she is with us and gets to experience it too. Immediately after Kailani's death, both Matt and I agreed that we would spread her ashes around the world; she would travel the world with us and together we would share these experiences.

For us, dead did not mean gone. It just means she is present in a different way. Attending that education session on grief and observing others who were stuck really motivated me to ensure I didn't struggle through this experience in the same ways. I gave myself permission to move forward with my grief and with Kailani.

I mean, yes, there are periods where my grief feels all-consuming and crippling, though these are not frequent or for long durations. I've been down that road in the past. I've experienced severe depression and isolation; it is not something I ever want to go through again. I know where that road leads, and it is dark and twisted, with little opportunity to be happy. And it is so incredibly difficult to crawl out of that space, though not impossible.

I would rather choose happiness. Not only for me, but for my daughter. Because if the roles were reversed, I would want my mom to live a happy, healthy, and fulfilled life. I would hope that the love we shared inspired and empowered her to be strong, brave, and resilient; just as I believe my little Kailani would want for me. I give myself permission to live in that version.

Therefore, I dedicated my time following her death to figuring out exactly how to cope with the death of our daughter. I work hard every day to find structure and routine that allows joy and grief to coexist within my life. It is not easy, and life continues to be a challenge every single day. There is not a single second in the day that passes that I don't yearn for my baby girl and have this constant hole in my heart. Yet some days are filled with joy, while other days are filled with grief and mourning. And that is okay.

So, I started exploring different methods to help guide me through my grief and assist in my healing. I share these as a way to inspire and empower others in their grieving and healing journeys. This is not meant to be a "you must," "you need," or "you will" type of list. These are activities that I have welcomed into my life to help create a balance of joy and sorrow within my day-to-day activities. Remember, we all do grief differently. So, take what works, and leave what does not. Never feel the need to apologize or suppress what you are feeling. You do grief the way that works for you. Feel your grief in whatever way it shows up for you. Just know that however that looks, whatever it feels like for you, is perfect.

Talk About It

- Having a community or group of individuals to share my story with has been one of the most therapeutic means for managing my grief. With access to today's technology, there are so many opportunities to connect with others who've experienced similar situations and have insights to share.
- Initially, I wasn't interested in counselling services or attending a grief support group; however, these are some things I have tried. The grief group allowed me to connect with and meet individuals who were more local to me, although they did not share the same experience of neonatal loss. I have also connected with different counsellors and have found two specific criteria to be critical in building my relationship with these professionals:

  > a.) Knowledge and experience with what I am experiencing. For example, I was not interested in speaking to a counsellor who specializes in substance use about my neonatal loss.

  > b.) The vibe they give off and the connection between the individual and me. Sometimes people just don't jive, and that is okay. Just know that each professional's approach is different, and it may take a couple of trials before you find the right fit.

Permission to Grieve

- Society seems to have built up specific expectations and timelines around grief. However, know that you, like me and everyone else, are not expected to work through your grief in any type of specific linear progression. There is no timeline to place on grief, and grief is not limited to five stages, as identified and discussed in various books and resources. One experiences an array of thoughts and feelings in one's loss, all of which are completely individual. My grief and my grieving process are different from what others might experience, and that is *okay*.

- Know that this is *your* experience and give yourself permission to grieve in a way that is most supportive to you and your needs.
- Carve time into your day to simply grieve, whatever that looks like for you. If that means crying for x amount of time, then do so. Allow yourself what you need to move into your grief and forward in your healing.

Give Back

- I have found that one of the most rewarding and meaningful ways to bring happiness and fulfillment to my life is by giving back and helping others. With that said, following Kailani's death, Matt and I knew that many of our friends and family would want to send us flowers, gift baskets, etc. Instead of this, we requested that individuals donate toward the hospital and the unit that supported us through this challenging time in our lives.
- We set up a trust in memory of Kailani to support the education, recruitment of staff, and purchase of equipment to aid these units so they can further provide the knowledge, support, and resources needed to ensure other families are taken care of through their pregnancy journey. We also hope that this will further support and decrease the occurrence of pregnancy and infant death rates.
- Knowing gifts are being provided as a tribute to our daughter means the world to us. Furthermore, it helps ensure her memory is carried on. Helping others in need makes us feel like her life and our experience holds a greater purpose and is contributing to the advancements and awareness of PAIL.

Practice Gratitude

- Now, I know, for many individuals, trying to be grateful during times of mourning and grieving is no easy task. Note that you do not need to direct your gratitude toward the death of your loved one or the experience. It may start with something like having access to clean water, shelter, or clothes. Over time, you may find things start to connect with your experience. For example, I was initially really upset and angry that diagnostics stated that Kailani's scans were normal. However, if we had known the situation earlier in the pregnancy, I do not know if we would have ever made it as far along in our pregnancy and been able to spend those twenty minutes with our baby girl.
- The benefits of practising and implementing gratitude into one's life are significant. Most importantly, it helped me to recognize that not everything in my life was miserable. Gratitude helped to lighten the weight of my grief.
- The first resource that placed me on the path of practising gratitude daily is the book *The Magic* by Rhonda Byrne. Her book takes individuals on a twenty-eight-day gratitude journey, and I can honestly say it has been one of the most impactful books I have ever read. I go through this practice in my Raising Resilience Movement group on Facebook.
- For those who feel this could be a bit overwhelming, the other resource I use every morning and evening is *The Five Minute Journal.*
- Note, gratitude practices can look different for everyone. It can start by taking a moment out of your day to say or write down the items that you are grateful for.

Mindfulness

- Going for a walk has been one of the best ways to step away from my life and just allow myself to be. I invite individuals to consider walking outside in a nature-filled space; the fresh air and connection it provides are incredibly therapeutic. Do not think about the dishes that need to be done or other endless lists of tasks on your to-do list. Just simply allow yourself to be in that moment.
- This time was also a means for me to reflect. Some individuals find that sitting in a quiet area, closing their eyes, and focusing on their breathing is the only means of meditation. However, the purpose of meditation is to practice mindfulness, which can be done through various activities. Walking is one of those activities for me. I invite you to carve time out of your day and allow yourself the opportunity to practice mindfulness or mindful stillness and turn your attention internally.
- Consider exploring mindfulness and stillness practices available on different social media platforms.

Memorials

- Having items throughout the house that represent Kailani has been extremely important to me and part of my healing process. Alternatively, individuals might prefer having a dedicated memorial space or area in their house versus items throughout.
- I felt the need to have many items throughout the house:
    - o Stuffed elephant (Smudge) and the book *Love You Forever* in my bedroom, duplicates of the same items cremated with Kailani.
    - o Pink vase in my kitchen, which held the flowers I received while in the hospital.

- o Bonsai tree in my office, representing growth, harmony, peace, and balance. I purchased it following Kailani's death.
- o Angel wing macramé – I have a set in my office as well as one in the nursery. I want our future children to know that they will always have their sister watching over them; that is, if we are gifted with future children though I acknowledge that this isn't guaranteed.
- Gravestone and site
  - o For many individuals, this helps them in their mourning and grief as it allows them an opportunity to go and be present with their loved one.
  - o This might be the location where an individual's body has been buried or where the individual's ashes have been released or buried.
- Plant a tree, flower, or other seedling
  - o There is the opportunity to have a loved one's ashes mixed in with the soil of a plant to support its growth and have their ashes contribute to the life of the foliage.
  - o Some funeral homes might have a tree planted in honour of the deceased as part of their services. Kailani has one that will be planted in Calgary in the spring of 2021.
- Jewellery, ornaments, and other memorabilia
  - o I have different ornaments and décor that represent Kailani for different times of the year. Halloween = white pumpkin with pink stem, Christmas = angel wings.
  - o There are artisans and jewellers who combine the ashes of loved ones and make them into blown glass ornaments, glass jewellery, metal jewellery, and even stones, such as birthstones and diamonds.

- There is a wide variety of miscarriage and memorial jewellery available on various sites such as Amazon and Esty.
  - I wear an angel wing necklace with the letter K that was gifted to me by my sister-in-law.

Journal

- Journaling and writing about my experience have proven to be very beneficial. I admit it has not always been easy. Reliving the experience over and over again is very emotional. Also, I am not proud of some of the thoughts and feelings I had during this time. However, journaling allowed me the opportunity to reflect and release my thoughts and emotions to support my healing journey.
- Some may find it beneficial to keep a journal that is separate from others they may have. After connecting with others who've experienced similar situations, they've opted to burn these once they moved through their grief.
- Some journaling prompts that I have found helpful:
  - What will you do for yourself today?
  - How are you feeling today?
  - Self-care ideas list – refer back to as needed.
  - What did you learn about yourself today?
  - What three things are you grateful for today and why?
  - What do you wish people would say/wouldn't say to you?

Explore Your Spirituality

- Prior to my pregnancy and this whole experience, I struggled to connect with my spirituality. However, there are ways in which I've been able to explore this more:
    - Spend more time in nature; take time to appreciate and take in everything in my environment. This has allowed me to feel more connected to something greater than myself.
    - Numerology was something that was of interest to me and led me down a path to discover angel numbers and sequential patterns in my life.
    - Following the death of our daughter, I found solace through the use of angel tarot cards and their positive messages.
    - Meditation has continued to be a challenge for me, although I am slowly becoming more attuned with my inner self and have granted myself permission to feel whatever it is I am feeling or thinking.
    - Books have allowed me to discover new perspectives and beliefs. I found a series by a hypnotherapist named Michael Newton and found comfort in the client sessions he shared about life between lives. Through his readings and those of others, I ended up developing my own beliefs around life, death, and source that have provided me with comfort and a new understanding of my life and purpose.

Explore Your Creativity

- For me, painting has always been a way for me to relax and express myself in a way that I did not feel I could do verbally. Each of us is a creative being, even when we think we are not.

Creativity does not require the creation of something specific. It can simply mean taking paint to a surface or using whatever material one feels most connected to and allowing whatever happens to happen. Allow this to be an opportunity where there is no expectation and no judgment. Just allowing oneself to enjoy the process and embrace it can be therapeutic and healing.

- Though painting is my primary creative outlet, I also have explored the following activities:
    o Macramé
    o Making a journal for building healthy habits
    o Wood working (desk, shelving, etc.)
    o Creating a cover for this book
    o Indoor gardening
    o Content creation for social media
- Honestly, there are no limits to exploring one's creative side. Cooking and baking are also things that many individuals enjoy. Myself, I am more into the eating part, so it is best if I stay out of the kitchen.

Exercise

- Now, I know I listed walking above. I thoroughly enjoy taking a stroll without exerting myself; therefore, I do not consider my walks to be a form of exercise. However, it is movement that is important.
- There are so many different types of exercise out there, and the benefits of exercise are long and well known by most, so I will not go into that here. However, what I will say is that exercise does not have to be a chore. Yes, you read that right. Exercise can be fun. Often it is thought that exercise means going to the gym or spending an hour on an elliptical, though that is not the case. Exercise comes in many forms and can be done in a variety of settings. Explore what works best for you.

- If you do not know where to start, maybe consider exploring an exercise class or trainer. Note, these do not need to be done in person. I did a couple of thirty-day challenges with a trainer from New York. I didn't have to create a workout routine or anything. I simply had to show up. Also, paying for a service or having an accountability buddy makes all the difference for me.
- Oh, LaCara, I just don't have the time! This is something I would tell myself frequently. However, thirty minutes a day is all it takes. That leaves me with twenty-three and a half hours left in a day to do all the things. Also, I am going to leave you with these two thoughts:
    1. If you don't make time for your health right now, you will be *forced* to make time for your illness.
    2. Stop bingeing on Netflix and social media. (I am guilty.)
    3. I know, I know, I said two. Though I just thought of another thing . . . once I made health a priority in my life, I found the time. Make your health a priority.
- I look at it like this: if others can juggle kids, cooking, working full-time, plus having a side hustle, etc., then it is possible for me to do it, too. Therefore, I had to stop making excuses and get it done. I found myself feeling better, having a much more productive day, and experiencing so many more benefits. Remember, exercise doesn't have to be a chore, and it doesn't have to be done alone. Personally, I am very competitive, so seeing Matt's activity on my watch just motivates me that much more.

Write a Letter to Your Loved One

- So many times, we hear people say, "I wish I could have told them . . ." However, I want to invite individuals to consider a different perspective on this. Our relationships with those who have died do not simply come to an end. I invite you to think about this. What if there is the possibility that they are listening to us, watching over us, etc? Personally, I did not take on certain religious beliefs growing up. However, the experience of having our daughter die shortly after birth inspired me to do some self-discovery into my spirituality. This led me to develop new beliefs around life and death. Therefore, I choose to believe that I am still able to talk to Kailani. I choose to believe that she hears my voice, and I can feel her presence. And for that reason, I can talk to her whenever I want and tell her all the things.

- Putting things on paper allows us to let it out and is a means to express ourselves. After the death of my best friend's dad, she told me she regretted never being able to tell him certain things. So, I asked her to write a letter and address it to him. The feedback I received from her was positive, and she said it truly helped her in more ways than she expected. It actually strengthened her spirituality and the connection she felt with her dad, even though he was no longer here with us.

- For me, I've chosen to believe that death does not mean gone. Therefore, I feel this ongoing connection to my little girl and know that she is listening and watching over me. Again, you get to choose.

Reading

- I have always been a fan of books. I love reading. Hence, when Kailani died, I was rather disappointed that I could not find a selection of books to help me through PAIL. Over time, I have discovered that there are books out there, though they are not widely available, and many are self-published and offered through certain organizations/initiatives that support PAIL. It wasn't until four or five months into my journey that I became aware of many of them.

- Reading is a great activity to stretch and exercise the mind. I also found it to be a good outlet, providing me a break from my grieving. Give yourself permission to take a break. For a long time, I felt that I must grieve 24/7. Although this is not mandatory, we are allowed to give ourselves a break, whatever that might look like for us.
- Mix it up. I typically read books that are more educational and focus on health, wellness, and business. During my grieving, I found it better to mix things up. I have always been obsessed with personal growth and development, so I often avoid what I call leisure reading. However, post-Kailani, I decided to mix things up and expand my horizons. I invite others to consider trying something new. You never know what you might find out there that sparks a new interest or passion.

Take a Bath

- I have never been a person who enjoys baths. However, I decided to follow the post-delivery recommendations of taking a bath. Turns out, they aren't so bad.
- Initially, I did this because it helped with my muscle aches and was encouraged as part of my post-delivery healing. Over time, I grew to enjoy taking baths.
  - o I used this as an opportunity to unwind and simply be. During my bathing, I often would meditate, listen to music, read a book, listen to a podcast, or simply stare off into space. Sometimes I would sit in the bathtub and cry for an hour straight. Whatever I needed, I just did that. Do whatever you need.
- Now for those not well experienced with the luxuries that bathing can provide, a word from the now-experienced. If you're wanting to take your bathing experience to the next level, I might invite you to explore the use of bath bombs, essential oils, Epsom

salts, etc. (once post-delivery healing is complete and depending on your health and wellness specifications).

- Side note, for those with muscle aches and pains: I found stretching is best after a bath as this helps to loosen up those muscles. Remember to take care of all aspects of you.

A SERIES OF FIRSTS

F ollowing the loss of a baby comes a series of firsts: the first time we enter the nursery, the first time we see a pregnant woman, the first time we hear a baby cry. The list is endless. In addition to being part of a series of firsts, these are often items and situations that are triggering to our realities and our grief. However, there is a series of firsts that do not occur on a regular day-to-day basis, like those triggers such as a baby's cry, pregnancy announcements, etc.

I am talking about the first time we return to work, and the first time someone asks, "How is your baby?" The first Christmas without Kailani. Her first "would have been" birthday. Those events that come maybe once a year but are heavy on our hearts and feel crippling to our souls.

I remember waking up on September 20, 2020, and feeling like there was a heaviness in the air. Matt and I were heading to the family lake house to pack, as it had recently sold. The drive there was about an hour and a half from our house. For most of the drive, I sat in silence, thinking about our sweet little girl. I thought, *Does he even know what day it is?* He didn't say a word. I received a couple of messages that morning from loved ones asking if I was okay.

Of course, I had become accustomed to applying the acceptable answer we provide to others within our society; "I am fine" was my response. In reality, my heart was broken, and I felt empty. My soul felt dark. I wanted to stay in bed and cry. Instead, I cried silently in the passenger seat while we drove the distance. Why, you ask? Because September 20, 2020, was my due date.

Reflecting back to this day, I am grateful for what felt like hours of driving. It allowed me the space I needed to express my grief prior to seeing others in my family that day. I honestly wanted to stay in bed and have myself a pity party. However, once I got to work packing boxes and cleaning, I found that I was able to spend quite a bit of time thinking about my sweet baby girl Kailani while I also worked toward some type of goal. That felt good.

It was at that moment I discovered there was a way for me to overcome this series of firsts. It was not through distracting myself or avoiding the day or succumbing to a pity party. It was by allowing and creating a space where I could grieve my baby girl while also doing something productive and moving toward some type of goal. Having a goal in place allowed me to take my energy and apply it in a way that was supporting my body, mind, and soul.

Before I move forward and discuss how I managed through many of my firsts, I feel it important to highlight how this approach assists in healing the body and mind at a fundamental level. Note how I incorporated the grieving process and did not suppress or avoid these feelings; this is important.

Facing the Holidays

Okay, I am going to take you back to that fight or flight response that our bodies experience during times of stress. Stick with me for a bit, as I am going to break this down a bit further and yes, I know we went over it. Seriously, LaCara, like how many times are you going to go over this?! However, there is a reason they say that "Repetition is the mother of skill."

The fight, flight, and freeze response is our body's way of responding to a stressful situation and results in a change to how our bodies operate in that moment. This can be triggered not only through a physical threat, but also through our own internal thoughts and feelings.

For many of us, when we are faced with our first Halloween, Thanksgiving, Christmas, or birthday after the death of a loved one, our mind triggers the stress response and we may start to experience the same symptoms we would have if we were facing a dangerous or scary situation.

We may feel anxious at the thought of having to face these holidays. Maybe our blood pressure rises, our heart rate increases, and our breathing changes. Maybe we begin to feel nauseated or lightheaded. And then we think to ourselves, *F*** no, I am not doing X, Y, or Z. I am staying in bed. Today is not happening. I refuse to acknowledge that it is (insert holiday).* I tried this approach, and as a result, it made me feel so much worse. I began to feel as though I was further suppressing Kailani's memory by not incorporating her memory and existence into these special holidays.

I thought by doing so I would be able to avoid the pain that celebrating these holidays might bring without her being present. I thought that if I skipped over these firsts or eliminated them from my life, I could create just another day. However, the truth is, every day is painful. One week, one month, two months, four months, even years down the road, that pain is going to be there, and so many families can attest to this. The hole we have and that pain we experience is never going to go away. Every day without our babies is heartbreaking and soul shattering. However, we have an opportunity. We can give ourselves permission to make things easier on ourselves. Although, I must admit, it is not necessarily without a challenge.

I mean, I certainly did not come out with my fists up and guns blazing in fighting mode. Instead, I took the position and the belief that my baby is with me every step of the way. Instead of avoiding the holidays, Matt and I celebrate them and include our daughter within our traditions. Not only that, I worked to create new traditions that were inspired by her, which have supported us in our grieving journey. This allowed me to take inspired action and help my body transition out of the fight, flight, and freeze mode that I so often found myself in. I absolutely love this quote that I came across:

> *"Those we love don't go away; they walk beside us every day. Unseen, unheard but always near. Still loved, still missed, and held so dear." – Author Unknown.*

This is the quote that I wrote, as part of an angel card exchange, in over thirty Christmas cards to families who have experienced pregnancy or infant loss. This was the first year I have ever done a card exchange and to be honest, if I hadn't gone through this experience, I likely would have gone my entire life without participating in one. I spent days on these cards. I even spent half a day trying to come up with a meaningful poem to include in these cards to add that personal touch. Then, when I signed the cards, I included my sweet baby girl Kailani and placed an oval above the last "i" in her name to represent a halo. Writing her name on those cards brought a sense of peace and pride to me. It heightened the connection I felt to others and is now that special something that my baby girl and I get to do as a new holiday tradition.

As I take on and create new traditions for the various holiday seasons, I actually feel a sort of excitement. I find myself asking, "In what ways can I heighten Kailani's presence during this holiday season?"

As Thanksgiving in Canada comes before Halloween, I painted white and pink pumpkins in remembrance of Kailani and brought one as a centrepiece to my mom's house for dinner. This was also part of our décor for Halloween.

I make sure that Kailani has a presence in everything we do, and I take every opportunity to create new and meaningful ways to ensure exactly that. Why? Because my baby girl may not be here in human form, though she lives on through me. In my heart and in my soul. Her life has impacted me to the core and changed who I am. Therefore, she is not gone; she is present in a different way.

I am not going to lie and say that I do not experience triggers during the holiday seasons, because that is far from the truth, though

I do my best to practice patience and compassion toward myself and toward others. For example, an individual that I took a business course with posted a picture of her daughter dressed as a ghost/angel for Halloween. I didn't comment or anything on the picture, though I had a wide variety of thoughts and words going through my head at that moment. *Why on Earth would you dress your baby as a ghost/angel when so many of us face this actual reality?*

Then I noticed just how much it impacted me. I had a cloud over my head for a week following Halloween and ended up talking to my counsellor about it. Lo and behold, I learned that Halloween is a challenging holiday for many parents with angel babies.

I was so angry for that week; so angry. Though, when I really think about it, these situations have always been present. The reality is, I would not have thought twice about that picture in the past, prior to this experience. I mean, dressing a child up at Halloween is what people do. I can think of some Halloween outfits I wore as a child that would have been considered offensive to others. But children and parents don't usually sit down and consider the pros and cons of how their outfit may be received by other people, based on those people's experiences or values and beliefs. At least, I should say, the majority of individuals do not do this. In all honesty, if Kailani had been here for Halloween, I would have been just as excited to dress my little "angel" up. I mean, why wouldn't I want to dress her up and celebrate Halloween, like I've done throughout my life?

Other people's actions and behaviours are not (usually) aimed at offending or harming others. It is our experiences that have changed the way we view these situations. Unfortunately, because our perspective and experiences have changed, we must work to mould it even further. By moulding our minds, we can decrease the negative impact that these types of situations have on us and allow ourselves the opportunity to move forward through these triggers without allowing a dark cloud to take over for weeks at a time. Yes, they will likely still trigger us. However, we can prevent that weeklong cloud that hovers over us and makes us the queen/king of misery for that period. This is best done by gaining new perspectives and exercising understanding and compassion.

The truth is that people do not often think about their actions or how they impact those around them. I have been guilty of this, and I am sure each of you reading this has been guilty of this at some point or another in your life. However, if we can come to terms with this, it truly can support and further facilitate our own health and wellness.

Prior to this experience, many of these triggers were just something that were part of my day-to-day or annual routine. I didn't think twice about things and, fortunately, many individuals will never understand how these types of situations impact others because they have not gone through the same experience. Truly, I hope they never have to. However, as we move forward in sharing our own stories and talking about these triggers, we can begin to support change and produce an internal dialogue within those around us by creating awareness.

Facing Coworkers

Now, the other big "first" I experienced was returning to work and facing all the people in that environment. I don't think I fully disclosed to everyone what I do, though I work in healthcare, and prior to taking some time off from work, I was in a managerial role, working at our local health authority. Therefore, not only did I have to face coworkers and friends, but I also had to face the healthcare system and the programs that work with babies and their families.

So what the heck is a person to do? Well, first off, my online group, the Raising Resilience Movement, was a great way to share information, as I had some coworkers following my journey on that platform. That meant I didn't have to tell my story multiple times as people already knew; they didn't need to ask. However, not all my coworkers were in this group.

I admit, the first time I went into the office, it was a struggle. I've worked with many of these individuals for quite a long period of time and have developed strong connections with many of my coworkers and the staff in various units.

For some, my experience impacted them significantly. Emotions were high for a handful of individuals and, therefore, there were some tears to be shed when I encountered different individuals. Due to COVID-19, hugs and contact were not supported, and this helped me a bit. I am the type of person who can hold my emotions in pretty well, until someone hugs me. Then it is as though I absorb all their energy, and then I turn into a blubbering disaster.

Now, keep in mind, I made an effort to go into the office on a couple of different occasions to ease myself back into this environment. This was done in an attempt to decrease feeling completely overwhelmed and lessen the impact of people wanting to connect with me all at once.

On one occasion, I went into the office to talk with my boss about some concerns I had about my return to work, recognizing that babies were a trigger for me. It just so happens that one of the departments I work with oversees the care of pregnant women, both pre- and post-partum. As I was coming into the office that day, I saw an individual I work with, and she said, very chipper, "Oh, you must have had your baby already. How's the baby doing?"

My heart sank. I managed to keep it together in that moment and said, "Yes, I did have my baby, though, unfortunately, she died." Of course, she looked devastated for asking, and it looked as though tears were filling her eyes. She apologized and said she wanted to cry. I simply told her that I've done enough crying for everyone and that sometimes life is just unkind.

Once I finished my meeting with my boss and made it back into my vehicle, I began to cry. Breathing became difficult and I wanted to scream. To be honest, those conversations are difficult and I don't feel like they get any easier over time. They bring forward my grief and a tsunami of emotions. What do I do in these moments? Well, I ride the wave.

I cried in my vehicle for about half an hour and just allowed all the feelings to hit me. The situation sucked. The reality is, there aren't many people in my life who've been in the position I am in. I cannot be angry with individuals for not knowing that my baby died. Yes, these conversations suck, and I guarantee it is uncomfortable for both parties. I know she didn't ask this as a means to hurt me or intentionally trigger my grief. Sometimes these types of situations occur, and that is just life. As a result, there are times when Matt and I must face these types of conversations, and they are painful. The only thing we can do is take them as they come and allow ourselves to feel whatever it is we feel. Over time, the frequency of these conversations lessen.

Now, of course, to assist with decreasing and eliminating these types of conversations, I went ahead and did something a little less conventional. I asked a co-worker to forward an email out to staff to thank them for their support and understanding while I navigated through my grief following Kailani's death. This helped create awareness within the different teams and decreased the chances of some awkward and painful conversations. However, I also recognized that it is a challenge to ensure everyone receives these updates and reads their emails.

Returning to Work

Okay, so this really isn't part of the series of firsts, though I do appreciate that concentration and focus can be extremely difficult and compromised when returning to work. Therefore, I want to take a moment and share a couple of tips/tricks that have helped me with my focus. Returning to work, especially in a position that requires a lot of brainpower, has been extremely challenging and at times has felt defeating.

The first step was recognizing my limitations. As I shared previously, I oversee areas that work with babies and, for me, this is a trigger. Over time, I know that I will be able to manage and cope with this more and more, though this is a sore spot for me. Therefore, I discussed my concerns with my manager as a way for us to collaborate and identify methods on how I might transition back into the role, anticipating there might be some bumps along the way. Fortunately, my manager was extremely supportive and understanding, which provided me the reassurance I needed to return to my position.

Second, my energy levels and ability to perform like I did prior to my experience were not the same. Therefore, I took the time to explore what options were available to me. This included a change in my position, a gradual return to work, the delegation of certain tasks, etc. The most important thing for me was to set things up to support my success in returning to work. This meant evaluating my role, my responsibilities, and my priorities while, again, recognizing and acknowledging my limitations and my abilities during this time and seeking appropriate support and resources to aid in transitioning back to work. Prior to everything, I considered myself a very high-functioning overachiever, so these modifications felt like I was somehow losing. However, it is important to recognize that things will improve as time moves forward. In the meantime, take it day by day.

Third, and possibly the most important, recognize that you have power in structuring your day. Historically, I did not take breaks and would work many additional hours. I would continue to work outside my working hours, and Matt would always comment about how I didn't put down my work phone in the evenings. My thought was, *If I do it today, then it will not be so busy tomorrow*; or, *If I deal with it now, I can put out the coals before it turns into a flame.* In reality, there is always work to be done, and it will be there the next day. No matter how many extra hours I put in, with each passing day, I was doing the exact same thing. Truth: time is something we never get back. I don't want my eulogy to say that I was married to my work or have a headstone that reads "workaholic, absent friend/wife/mother, etc." As a side note, I would never be buried as I fear bugs getting into any orifice of my body.

Regardless, what I am saying is this: Take breaks. Take time for you. Don't work yourself into the ground. The reality is, the work will be there tomorrow, and you and your health remain the priority. Truth be told, when I take breaks throughout my day, I am way more productive. In some countries, they actually set limitations on working hours, as studies have proven that working long hours and not taking breaks reduces productivity. Therefore, implement things that increase your productivity, like taking a break every thirty minutes and drinking water. Heck, why not walk over to the water cooler! Look at that: combining tasks and improving productivity already! #winning

Not only that, eliminate distractions in your environment. Have a deadline to meet? Turn off those email notifications and your phone for thirty minutes. One thing I discovered during this COVID-19 pandemic and working from home, I get so much more done when I am not in the office. Why? Because there are limited distractions at home. Therefore, create a space that is supportive of your concentration and productivity.

Remember, you must take care of yourself. If we do not take care of ourselves and fall ill, then work can become increasingly challenging, or we may not be able to do it at all. Be intentional with your time and remember that there are always consequences to actions.

• • •

Now, there are honestly a hundred other things that I could write about within the pages of this book. Though, I am continuing to learn as I go and this is just the beginning for me. In closing, I would like to leave you with a couple things.

First, I would absolutely love to hear from you and hear about your experiences. Please don't hesitate to reach out via social media or even join the Raising Resilience Movement group.

Second, I want to remind you that *you* get to determine how you carry your grief. You hold the power and can give yourself permission to move forward with your grief. You also get to determine how that might look for you. There is always the ability to adopt or change how this looks over time and as one moves forward in carrying the weight of their grief.

Third, *you* get to decide how to view this new world around you, recognizing that your experiences have a significant impact on how you see and do things now. The kindest thing I did for myself was taking brief moments in my day to acknowledge, allow, and give myself permission to experience all parts of my life differently. This included periods of highs and lows. I like to remind myself of this daily and use the following mantra:

> *I acknowledge, I allow, and I give myself permission to make changes to who I am and how I am, so I can grow into the person I envision myself to be. I acknowledge, I allow, and I give myself permission to make changes in how I work and live my life, so that I can live a life of happiness and fulfillment.*

Sometimes creating a little mantra to help us through each day can make a significant impact. The great thing is, we can change our mantra at any time as our experiences will change our thoughts, feelings, and goals moving forward.

Lastly, please remember that *you* do have power and control in your life. You can give yourself permission to move through your grief. You can give yourself permission to allow both grief and happiness to coexist in your life. A life with grief doesn't mean a life without happiness. A life with grief, means you experienced love.

Each of us has a unique opportunity and ability to impact those around us in a way that can aid others in gaining new perspectives and understandings of what it means to be a PAIL survivor. We all have the power to inspire change in a culture that doesn't fully understand, welcome, or accept grief. Together we can change the culture around pregnancy and infant loss.

Much Love and Light,
LaCara

PART 3

KEEPING THE MEMORIES ALIVE

FOREVER LOVED
AND CHERISHED

We remember the babies that were born sleeping; the babies that we carried and never held; the babies held but did not come home; and the babies who came home but could not stay.

- Author unknown

The job of an angel's mother is to keep her child's memory alive and we speak their names.

Antonietta Rota 10/12/1954	Baby Edge 02/19/1987	Derek Joseph Sundwall 10/12/1985
Mia Nuñez 10/21/2017	Ella Kinch 11/24/2016	Joey Louis Wocknitz 06/09/1978
Joseph Ervin Ziskovsky 03/18/2011	Maverick William Robinette 08/22/2020	Adeline Gloria Bell 05/30/2020 – 06/25/2020

Mary Grace 01/08/2020	Mason Lewis 09/22/2020	Madelyn Delores Rouh 12/13/2019 – 12/17/2019
Josiya 06/09/2020	Colton James Trefz 08/29/2020	Blake Redgrift 03/24/2018 – 03/26/2018
Cornell Qiang Zhang 04/21/2020	Ailiana Elizabeth Johnson 05/18/2020	Stratton Ray Gaylor 05/04/2020
Freya Khouas 10/08/2016	Heaven Khouas 07/02/2018	Emery Dakota Martin 03/16/2017
Tayten Day Hetue 05/03/2017	Hannah Patricia Green 08/09/2019 – 08/18/2019	Tiffany Anhorn 11/22/1988
Elisha Owen Hetue 02/28/2019	Payton Lee Prechel 01/14/2010	Coby Cleverly 08/23/2020
Celeste Love York 10/13/2020 – 10/18/2020	Allison Mary Prechel 08/01/2012	Delilah Reign Gutierrez 10/05/2018 – 11/17/2018
Dylan Albert Boyd 10/06/2004	Malorie Marie Mlenek 07/18/1999 – 10/11/1999	Mia Rose Whitehead 04/23/2009
Hanna Lucia Zajia 12/15/2020	Jaxson Kyle Shepherd 01/06/2017	Marlene Elmore 01/21/1979

FOREVER LOVED AND CHERISHED

Peyton Lee Havumaki 10/09/2008	Tyler James Johnston 06/01/1994 – 06/10/1994	Mackenzie Rose 09/19/2020
Lucah George Green 10/21/2019 – 06/10/2020	Jace Ronie Mullins 07/13/2020	Micah Edward Bennett 02/19/2018
Talan James Laue 09/25/2017	Stacey Rhona Lightbody 18/05/1980	Alwynn Lightbody 03/10/1982
Maverick Paul Feidt 09/11/2019	Theresa Ann Zylka 09/03/1982	Baby Girl Meyer 03/1999 Baby Boy Meyer 08/2001
Brinlee Jean Feidt 12/31/2019	Jude Tyler Roepke 10/05/2019 – 12/28/2019	Arrianna Rae Jones 01/18/2006 – 07/22/2006
Patrick Andrew Hallin 03/28/2001	Ryuie Kenshin Trinidad 05/06/2018	Jackie Dalena Dines 03/05/2002
Skylar Etta Anderson 04/19/2020	Andrew Steven Basinger 06/24/1991 – 07/04/1991	Kylie Brianna Comia Millanar 06/02/2020
Kyleigh Grace Shaw 08/31/2019	Leighton 05/20/2019	Randall 08/21/2020
Harry Palmer 04/06/2011	Omi Ryan Anthony 10/04/2020	Rylin Grimm-Hart 03/21/2018

Ryan William Sampson 01/27/2008	Artemis Baldr Cole 09/07/2015 – 12/08/2015	Chase Taylor Bethman 04/20/1998 – 04/21/1998
Johnathon Michael 06/30/2011	Chloe Louise Groselose 06/24/2007	Zane Allen Mason 03/24/2018
Beau Robert Schley 12/17/2019	Riley Schley 10/30/2020	Aspyn Olive Marquette 04/11/2018
Lexie Ava Frank 02/04/2020	Prince Neal 11/03/2012	Royal Neal 11/03/2012
Cali Rose Cavicchi 10/03/2020	Easton Alan Morgan 08/02/2020	Raelyn Faith Upchurch 01/13/2020 – 02/05/2020
Braanson Everett & Braeden Eugene Liess 07/2006	Kezyah Astra Grace Lies 10/21/2007	Esperanza Fonteyne Liess 11/28/2008
Taylor-Robin Gunner 10/28/2017	Ronnie Martin Keith Gunner 08/05/2019	Bailey-River Healion 09/11/2020
Gracie Leota LeeAnn Moreland 06/19/2020	Addyson Reign Latoya Jimenez 11/25/2020	Benton Travis Quamme-Kortan 08/27/2020
Elijah Alexander Perez 05/15/2016	Brinley Reese Freymann 11/06/2020	Eden Amanda Owens 08/07/2020

FOREVER LOVED AND CHERISHED

Elena Claire Brunell 12/07/2020	Juliana Rayne Goodin 07/30/2020	Lyra Maria Marianne Murphy 12/16/2019
Mila Caitlyn Jane Weddington 06/18/2020	Isla Pearl Ponchin 07/24/2020	Milo Emmett Palmer 04/24/20 – 04/28/2020
Carter Bentley Lehr 07/07/2016	William "Liam" Allen Gray, II 09/23/2020 – 11/30/2020	Jaxson Braylee Dabbs 07/26/2020 – 11/07/2020
Anthony Gambardella V 05/26/2020	Ava & Evie Pamment 11/05/2020	Johanna Claire Crawley, "JoJo" 02/04/2020
Korbin James 08/01/2019	Aletheia Hope Arete Gates 09/29/2017	Talitha Charity Mae Gates 06/09/2018
Douglas Ray Parker 08/20/2018 – 09/05/2018	Max Falk 11/28/2018	Selah Joy Guzman 01/07/2020
Valyn Brooks Wilhelm 06/05/2019	Delilah Reign Gutierrez 10/05/2018 – 11/17/2018	Bryson Asher Moore 11/18/2015
Haven Sky & Rylee Sage Jones 03/13/2017	Kelby Reign Jones 07/03/2018	Casey Louiz Serbando Cantrell 07/20/2005 – 12/09/2005
Sophia Claire Manning 10/05/2017	Rhys Moore 01/10/2020 – 01/11/2020	Emery Anahí Williams 07/28/2020

Jasmine Grace Cox 03/11/2018	Adam Daniel 21/06/1988	Lyric Eleine 07/04/2020
Rylie James Schultz-Saunders 06/11/2018 – 10/02/2018	Ashlyn Lee-ann Smith 06/24/2020	Bella Hurtado López 07/28/2020
Damieon Douglas Dickey 05/10/2018 – 06/28/2018	Emerson William McCarthy 11/29/2020	Maverick Je'Vaughn Edwards 03/12/2020
Oskar 04/17/2019	Gabriel Michael Yriarte 03/07/2020	Sophia LeAnn 03/31/2019
Harper Nicole Knox 09/01/2020 – 09/18/2020	Ayden Courdell- Edwards Thompson 10/22/2009 – 07/14/2010	Delainey Christine Davis 04/15/2020
Johnathan Prince Moch 04/13/2020	Jessy Lee Maynard Jr. 05/26/2020	Levi Jay Layton 05/17/2020
Willow Grace Centis 03/10/2020	Everlee Raelynn Cordes 07/03/2020 – 07/29/2020	Alijah Lee Riggs 02/22/2020
Adeline Gloria Bell 05/30/2020 – 06/25/2020	Elias Grant Kerrins 04/12/2020	Asyria Elizabeth Leggett 10/13/2016
Andrew Scott Wheeler 09/18/2009 – 10/01/2009	Keenan John Maxwell 01/12/2018	Journee Marie McGraw 02/05/2020

FOREVER LOVED AND CHERISHED

Sky Michael Wilson 06/01/2019	Kilian Vincent Lachmann 03/26/2018	Remington Sudol 07/19/2019
David Talon Pereira 09/08/2020	Mary Anne Cope 01/22/2015	Ashlynn Grace Sweatt 06/18/2013
Genevieve Annie Jewkes 04/22/2020	Nora Ann Adams 12/31/2019	Caden Jace Griffin 07/29/2020
Greyson Matthew Roland-McMahon 05/14/2020	Lucas Jeffrey Fox 06/09/2019	David Scott Arnburg 04/29/1989
Cooper Sky Seaton 03/12/2020	Brigham John Weaver 04/12/2018	Luca Araujo 11/23/2018
Ainsley Rose Wollf 09/01/2015	Ashlyn Grace Wilson 07/16/2016	James Joseph Perrella 01/23/2019 - 02/15/2019
Bella Rose Burnett 05/21/2015	Serriah Destinie Dobbins 04/03/2001	Gabriella Nicole Prichard 09/15/2018
Henry Allan Wayne Pack 11/14/2019	Jaxson Jude Dement 08/08/2020	Laci Jo Hill 11/04/2014
Baby Witt 08/01/2011	Ethan Dominic Peterson 02/23/2013	Raphael Tridimas 06/11/2020

Elijah Michael Gideon Niyonsaba 12/21/2019	Jameson Charles Carpenter 10/21/2020	Isaac Gabriel Watson 03/22/2012
Rylee Jane Hayhow 09/09/2020	Mina Josephine Herak 08/22/2020	Raegan Louise Brisentine 09/26/2019 – 10/06/2019
Galaxy Krystle Lotus Belanger 09/27/2015 – 08/17/2018	Matilda Bea Hunt 11/24/2020	Kaj Kristensen Bojen 01/09/2019
Robert James Pate 11/19/2019 – 11/18/2019	Madelyn Annette Johnston 09/15/2020	Remington Robert Shaw 08/08/2020
Tobias Milan Welch 10/15/2020	Karlie A.L.Regis 06/08/2019	Cassidy Jordon 01/16/2013 – 02/04/2013
Clara Elizabeth Johnston 10/18/2019	Calan Michael Tucker 09/01/2019	Nora Blain Walters 11/07/2019
Evelyn Marie 05/29/2020	Sam Joy Ritchson 12/18/2020 – 12/17/2020	Kinsley Karyn 12/29/2019
Madalynn Grace 05/03/2019	Sutton Rose Munsell 12/29/2019	Layne Marie Munsell 12/29/2019
Emma Alejandra Chocon-Andrade 05/30/2020	Aria Nicole Lopes 04/05/2017 – 12/04/2017	Henryk Kazimierz Kalinowski 11/06/2020

FOREVER LOVED AND CHERISHED

Mason John Scallan 02/06/2013	Elouise Suzana Begley-Emery 10/03/2014	Aubrey Jean Avery 03/01/2018 – 03/08/2018
Cameron Parker Burgess 06/10/1999	Roman Francisco Piche 08/30/2018	Carson Ryder 07/15/2020
Johnny James 07/01/2019	Presley Marie Smith 02/21/2019	Mark Anthony Madril 08/05/1965
Dominic Martin Legg 10/19/2017	Ellouise Rainier Rayman 08/11/2020	Harper Jean Jernigan 02/01/2020
Tucker James Waller 12/13/2019 – 12/16/2019	Tucker Simon-Paul Carpenter 06/27/2018 – 10/08/2019	Jurney Monae'Mills 07/25/2001
Isiah Prince Burton 07/26/2017	Maren Salinas Demars 07/25/2020	Waylon Alexander Montgomery 10/23/2020
Daniel Lee 09/19/2020	Paisley Joy Maranga 12/07/2020	Kaleb Nathaniel Isaiah Shifflett 07/26/2008
Alelia Ann Umland 11/07/2016	Baby Kevin 08/26/2000	Savannah Parker 10/08/2020
Alyssia Edwards 09/25/2006	Baby Jordan	Stella Kay Hall 07/08/2017 – 03/22/2018

Oakland James Brooks 03/31/2020	Kuhlekonke Sfundza 12/11/2020	Skylar Nicholas Wachsmuth 08/14/2001
Justin Tyrell 09/17/2017	Ariel Rose White 02/24/2019	Gideon Zuriel 09/02/2019 – 10/25/2019
Madalynn Elizabeth Allshouse 05/18/2018 – 01/01/2019	Camden Wayne Harris 11/16/2020	Levi Thomas Johnson 07/20/2019 – 10/03/2019
Jada Ann Mwaura 04/03/2019	Avery Quinn Cooper 01/20/2020	Karlee Mayebelle Jaxyn Taylor 04/15/2019
Everleigh Rose Rybak 12/14/2019	Gracelyn Louise Tusa 09/27/2017	Lauren Jaylie Foy 12/15/2019
Jessie Grayse Watson 06/30/2004 – 10/12/2004	Koray Andrew Cura Burtinshaw 08/08/2019	Alexandria Mersadies Whitley 11/15/2009
Miane van den Berg 08/02/2019 – 09/02/2019	Everett Chase Townley 01/14/2020	Hannah Nicole Wagamon 01/06/2000
Caleb Michael Strydom 02/18/2016	Charlotte Aletta Strydom 10/05/2017	Elijah Stevens-Matthews 02/10/2019
Monica Halsey Vasquez 10/21/2020 – 11/01/2020	Samuel James Cook 05/03/2020	Evan Nehemiah Camarillo 06/30/2020

FOREVER LOVED AND CHERISHED

Angel Baby Greget 2006	Addison Christene Kramer 10/26/2013	Carolyn "Cara" Mae Doane 08/20/2018 – 12/27/2018
Teddy Theodore Gordon Woodham 12/12/2020	Mirabelle D. Rivera 12/03/2019	Harmony Lyrical Webb 11/24/2017
Rónán LaRuche Rafter 11/12/2020	Willow Rosie Raj 08/11/2020	Noelle Grace Walters 12/26/2019 – 01/08/2020
Oliver James Kuppers 04/24/2018 – 05/06/2018	Eliza Rose 10/18/2019	Ajax Anthony Crocker 12/02/2020
Luka Stjepan Matkovic 02/12/2020	Ava-Grace Jane Kaveri 03/14/2018	Kehlani Oluwafunbi Adesuyi 08/16/2019 – 08/18/2019
Violet Sky 03/09/2020	Emma Juliette Tumale 02/12/2020	William R Hamilton 03/21/1975
Emily Rose Andrews 09/25/2014	Amelia-May 05/24/2019	Finley David Butler 11/11/2020
Aurora Julie Susan Hudson 04/11/2018	Everett Joseph Gatlin 02/13/2017	Lacey-mae 12/06/2019 – 21/01/2020
Angel Audrey Armstrong 07/25/2017	Kathleen Anne Marshall 07/27/2020	Joshua Lee Furlong 12/07/2005

Madison Melia Harvey 08/25/2012	Mason Malachi Lockwood 08/09/2018 – 08/11/2018	Connor MacSween 04/09/2019
Albert Stephen Cazier Jr. (AJ) 06/04/1994 – 09/19/1994	Aurora RosaLee Flores 08/29/2019 – 10/08/2019	Leighton Allen Jones 06/22/2017
Hadassah Esther Maria 08/23/2020 – 08/27/2020	Aiden Alexander Allred 03/31/2018	Malakeh Kanawati 06/03/2018
Makayla Lee Vass 05/11/2019	Stephanie Elizabeth Anne Seymour 11/30/2007	Bryan Austin Rogers-Irish 12/15/1995 – 01/11/1996
Mason Lewis Simpson 09/22/2020	Logan Michael Rossi 06/10/2018 – 06/22/2018	Bodhi Atom McLaggan 09/25/2020
Ferchel Hope Mendoza 07/28/2020 – 08/04/2020	Ruby Charlotte Jenkins 03/26/2018	Santino Gabriel Henderson 07/17/2013 – 07/19/2013
Bentley Owen Wallace 12/23/2019	Kamila Elizabeth 04/30/2015	Jaxon Kyle Melocheck 08/10/2018
Benjamin Pearsall V 11/18/2017 – 07/19/2018	Story Sophia Johnson 02/14/2020	Eleanor Esther Young 10/20/2020

FOREVER LOVED AND CHERISHED

Kalena Deena Ealy 05/13/2020	Kayson Edward Palmer 06/25/2020	Grayson Gregory Borchers 03/27/2019
Everett Thomas Ryan Dumas 09/20/2019 – 09/22/2019	Barston Ian Batchelder 12/04/2020	MarcAnthony Jack Yonnone 11/19/2018 – 01/27/2019
Ella Blake Morgan 09/05/2016	Alison Diana Phinney 11/01/2019	Lydia Rose Tarcau 03/23/2014
Kendall Gotong Mercado 01/10/2019	Layla Rose Love 05/07/2019	Hunter Eli Hellums 03/24/2018
Graycen Avery Hart 05/28/2020 – 05/30/2020	Elyse Riley Shelton 07/09/2020	Uno Bohara 11/23/2018
Mira Amia Heart Bohara 11/10/2020	Conner Anthony Johnson 04/11/2017	Drake Michael Radke 01/09/2017
Gabrielle Alexis Mattero 06/01/2011	Haley Lynn McCollum 06/12/2014	Camellia Kay Hill 07/30/2018
Luke Oliver Marlar 09/27/2016	Mayleigh Cheyenne Meyer 10/27/2019	Malachi Leal 11/29/2018
Ledger Lavon Moore 03/13/2020	Jack C. Young 09/06/2010	Grayson Norman Elliott 03/18/2017

Charlotte Jameson Atienza 11/14/2017 – 11/17/2017	Baby Robert Fallon 04/15/2020	David Darold Bowen 11/16/2020
Sandra Kay O'Connor 04/05/2020	Imogen Joan Spaeth 06/20/2018	Cornelia Ellery Gazaway 02/22/2018
Daniel Wesley Overby 05/27/2020	Salem Grace Hill 09/13/2020	Isadora Pelaez 08/16/2020
River Morgan 12/01/2020	America 05/28/2019	Ayla Aria Sue Tess-Hawkins 02/20/2020
Ivy Louise Lilly 07/05/2020	Colton James Trefz 08/29/2020	Jade Mackenzie Seadorf 12/30/2018 – 04/13/2019
Gwendolyn "Winnie" Ruth Melton 07/19/2015	Myah May 05/10/2017	Amairyah May 08/14/2019
Andrew Michael 05/07/1995	Angel Dubrova 04/07/2020	Cohen Lucas-William Christian 09/23/2016
Skye Elaine Callahan 02/10/2020	Raedyn Marcine Elder 12/13/2018	Leighton Oliver Alain Miller 12/20/2015
Hamish Buchanan 04/15/2020	Naama Borin 09/09/2020	Violet Celeste Chavez 01/16/2019

FOREVER LOVED AND CHERISHED

Elliott Malynn "Ellie May" Green 08/10/2017 – 09/07/2017	Jacob Ryan Setzer Jr. 05/28/2017	Emma Louise Gregory 02/03/1985
Jake William Michael Paul Brazier 12/14/2018	Coraleigh Ella Jayne Mullins 03/13/2018 – 03/20/2018	Carsen Ann Boyd 02/10/2019 – 02/12/2019
Joshua Charles Potthier 11/26/2018	Sierra Nicole Lewis 12/19/2002	Esme Rose Seraphina Fronda 04/14/2020
Dominic Philip William Musial 06/20/2016	Katarynna Chellnaeé-Rose Hazelwood 09/04/2020 – 08/17/2020	Trinity Lilianne Cusson 12/11/2020
Maimee - Rose Rodgers 08/13/2017	Jack Gargon Best 09/20/2019	Sally May Rose Best 09/26/2019
Sophia Lynn Deutsch 03/02/2016 – 03/06/2016	Samuel Colton Ellis 04/12/2017	Weston Garret Postpichal 01/01/2002
Evelyn Ellen Charlotte Dunn 05/08/2020	Baby D Douglas 05/2012	Ezikial Prince Semedo Douglas 05/12/2018
Baby J Douglas 04/2019	Emma Sarah Fowler 08/11/2019	Ruby Hope Baker 03/11/2015
Jace Thomas Baker 04/30/2020	Elijah Alexander Larsen 08/09/2013	Elena Rosalie Larsen 12/03/2014

LACARA BIDDLES

Stephen Alexander Larsen 04/27/2014	Kato Joe Edward Gross 09/22/2010 – 11/21/2020	Harleen Rhyn McCord 04/18/2017 – 09/05/2017
Leo James Mowery 02/01/2014	Nova Kennedy Stack 10/03/2020	Irma Yolanda Hernandez 03/29/1996
Zoey Von Martinez 08/16/2017 – 12/16/2017	Skyelar Jayde Reeves 10/10/2010	Spike Dragon Reeves 11/22/2012
Justin Jericho 06/21/2020	Jonah William Davis 03/12/2012 – 03/13/2012	Sophia Martha Davis 03/12/2012 - 03/17/2012
Anastasia McKown 10/05/2020	Reiden-James Sheehan 09/26/2020	Leon Ulric Barnett 09/25/2020
Calliope Grace Perlas 05/28/2018	Layla Hope Higgins 25/03/2018	Jasmine Lily Van Nimwegen 06/26/2019
Beau Maverick Martinez 12/14/2019	Dominic James Tayek 01/21/2019	Baby Boy Hurd 1969
Nthato Ntaopane 05/08/2018	Nevaeh Skye Goodrich 10/19/2020	Kenleigh Jo McDonald 01/26/2013
Catherine Rose Musch 02/15/2019 – 09/04/2019	Julianna Mary 11/05/2019	Christian Taylan List 12/23/2002

Lena Serenity Beauleau-Dube 12/05/2018	Zekial Leland Wagoner 08/28/2002	Jay Carrie Gage Jr. 01/24/2020 – 04/30/2020
Jayson Alexander Greene 12/17/2020	Grayson Nicholas Greene 12/17/2020	Kobi George Cousins 04/14/2019
Leo Arthur Tookey 03/02/2020	Harper Daniel Tookey 03/02/2020	Mila Grace Quinn 01/24/2020 – 05/21/2020
La'Darius Andre 06/15/2020	Biannca Lynn 06/15/2020	Jude Anthony Miller 09/12/2020
Lola Catalina Garza 03/10/2020	Patrick "Matthew" Prindiville Jr. 10/24/2020	'Ezeki'ela Alan Nahinu Vares 12/08/2020

Too Beautiful for Earth

I want to thank the mothers, fathers, grandparents, and families that have provided me the privilege of including the names of their babies as a way to honour their memory. We loved them for every moment of their existence, and that love will carry on forever.

RESOURCES

F or an up-to-date list of PAIL resources, please visit:
https://lacarabiddles.com/resources/

Angel Names Association

Angel Names Association (ANA) is a non-profit, charitable organization based out of New York that provides a wide variety of services to individuals and families who've experienced stillbirth. Their programs also support those who've experienced pregnancy loss or infant death.

Services offered, though are not limited to (must be a US resident):
- support for families and care providers
- financial assistance for end-of-life expenses
- grief education programs
- memory boxes
- raising money for stillbirth research

mgmosca@msn.com
https://angelnames.org/index.html

Angel Whispers Baby Loss Support Program

This Alberta based program inspires hope and healing and offers compassion and understanding to families devastated by the loss of a baby.

Services offered, though are not limited to:

- care packages (sent internationally)
- one on one grief support
- monthly baby loss support group
- monthly miscarriage support group
- monthly subsequent pregnancy support group
- quarterly newsletter
- annual grief retreat

angelwhispers@familiesfirstsociety.ca
www.angelwhispers.ca/angelwhispers
www.facebook.com/angelwhispersbabylosssupportprogram

Bridget's Cradles

Bridget's Cradles is a 501(c)(3) non-profit organization that donates cradles to hospitals in all fifty states across the United States. Based in Wichita, Kansas, it was created following the birth of Matt and Ashley Opliger's stillborn daughter, Bridget Faith.

This organization designs, creates, and distributes knit and crocheted cradles to hospitals across the United States, which provide a comforting way for bereaved families to hold their stillborn babies following delivery. These beautiful handmade pieces allow the baby to be cuddled gently in a cradle and provide opportunity for photographs and memories to be captured in a comforting and dignified way.

Bridget's Cradles also leads Christ-centred support groups, called *Hope Gatherings*, both online and in person at their headquarters in Kansas. Annually on October 15, Pregnancy & Infant Loss Remembrance Day, they organize an event called *Wave of Light* for families grieving their baby in Heaven. Bridget's Cradles also provides hope-filled resources and support on their website, including but not limited to:

- memorial ideas for honouring a baby in Heaven
- pregnancy loss quotes and Bible verses
- ways to navigate and celebrate important dates and holidays (e.g., due date, Heaven Day, Christmas)
- ideas on how to support a friend or family member who has experienced pregnancy or infant loss

info@bridgetscradles.com
www.bridgetscradles.com
www.facebook.com/bridgetscradles
Instagram: @bridgetscradles @ashleyopliger

Center for Loss in Multiple Birth, Inc. (CLIMB)

CLIMB is a non-profit organization based in Anchorage, Alaska, that serves families in any country who have experienced the death of one or more of their twin or higher-order multiple-birth children. It is a group of parents who have experienced the loss of one or more multiples, from the time of conception through childhood, and aim to share their stories to support and educate others on the realities and impacts of losses in multiple birth.

Services offered, though are not limited to:

- parent contact list
- sharing of stories and experiences

- education for relatives, friends, and health professionals
- newsletter
- Facebook support group for members

https://www.climb-support.org/

Empty Arms

This non-profit organization, located in Saskatoon, Saskatchewan, supports individuals and families experiencing grief following the death of a child. This includes individuals who've experienced the death of a child during pregnancy or after, up to children the age of six.

Services offered include, though are not limited to:
- neonatal end-of-life services
- online and in-person support groups
- in-hospital service support
- remembrance and photography keepsakes
- emotion and grief support
- postpartum support
- lactation support

https://www.emptyarmspls.com/
info@emptyarmspls.com
https://www.facebook.com/emptyarmsyxe

Infants Remembered in Silence (IRIS)

This non-profit organization, based out of Minnesota, provides support and education to individuals and families from the time knowledge is gained about the death of the baby, through to the funeral service.

Services offered include, though are not limited to:
- IRIS advocacy program

- bereavement support packets
- clothing sets
- common burial site options
- annual service of remembrance

support@irismembers.com
www.irisRemembers.com
https://www.facebook.com/InfantsRememberedinSilence

Molly Bears

This organization was created following the loss of Molly Christine. Her mother, Bridget, aims to support other grieving families by making weighted bears that equal the weight of the baby lost. Order forms are available on a monthly basis, and requests can be made for the creation of your Molly Bear, worldwide. See website for pricing.

admin@mollybears.org
https://mollybears.org/
https://www.facebook.com/MollyBearsOrg

Mommies Enduring Neonatal Death (MEND)

MEND is a Christian-based non-profit organization that is located in Texas. They offer support to those families who have experienced a miscarriage, stillbirth, or early infant loss and empower individuals to create a legacy from their children's lives.

Services offered include, though are not limited to:
- bi-monthly magazine
- commemorative ceremonies

- virtual support groups
- resources to support the grieving journey

rebekah@mend.org
https://www.mend.org/
https://www.facebook.com/MENDInfantLoss/

Perinatal Hospice and Palliative Care

This is a clearinghouse of information about perinatal hospice and palliative care for parents and caregivers, including health professionals.

Services offered include, though are not limited to:

- resources to support parents on their journey
- educational resources and content
- professional networking
- national and international listings providing perinatal hospice and palliative care
- families' stories

https://www.perinatalhospice.org/contact
https://www.facebook.com/PerinatalHospice/

Return to Zero: HOPE

This is a national non-profit organization based out of California. RTZ: HOPE aims to support the healing of families following PAIL while also creating a global impact by transforming the culture and stigma that currently exists around PAIL.

Services offered include, though are not limited to:

- support to parents, friends, family, and healthcare providers
- holistic healing retreats
- educational materials and training

- advocacy support
- online community

connect@rtzhope.org
https://rtzhope.org/
https://www.facebook.com/rtzhope

The Haven Network

An independent Christian ministry located in Northern Illinois, this perinatal hospice and bereavement center supports families who have experienced the death of a baby through ectopic pregnancy, SIDS, stillbirth, or miscarriage. In addition to these families, they also provide support to families who are facing a terminal diagnosis of their unborn or newborn child.

Services offered include, though are not limited to:
- bereavement materials
- books on newborn loss and grief
- in-hospital services
- hospice care
- grief support
- professional resources
- resource lists
- jewellery and memorial
- children support services
- financial resources

https://www.thehavennetwork.org/
info@thehavennetwork.org
https://www.facebook.com/thehavennetwork

ABOUT THE AUTHOR

LaCara Biddles is a registered nurse, transformation coach, course creator, and author who holds a BSc in Nursing from the University of Victoria, in addition to an MSc in Nursing from the University of British Columbia.

Through her personal losses and working as a palliative care nurse, LaCara has been provided with an intimate look into the realities faced by families following the death of a loved one. She truly realized how loss impacts every aspect of one's life, the harsh realities of grief, and the truth to navigating life following the loss of her baby, Kailani Mary Randall.

LaCara lives with her husband, Matt, in a remote and rural part of British Columbia, tucked away in the mountains. They remain hopeful that the future will bring them another child, while currently enjoying the company of their black lab, Gibson.

CPSIA information can be obtained
at www.ICGtesting.com
Printed in the USA
BVHW052251151221
624016BV00016B/1741